Copyright © 2024 by Blaze X. Maverick (Author)

All rights reserved. This book or any portion thereof may not be reproduced or used in any manner whatsoever without the express written permission of the publisher except for the use of brief quotations in a book review.

This book is copyright protected. This is only for personal use. You cannot amend, distributor, sell, use, quote or paraphrase any part or the content within this book without the consent of the author. Please note the information contained within this document is for educational and entertainment purposes only. Every attempt has been made to provide accurate, up to date and reliable complete information. No warranties of any kind are expressed or implied.

Readers acknowledge that the author is not engaging in the rendering of legal, financial, medical or professional advice. The content of this book has been derived from various sources. Please consult a licensed professional before attempting any techniques outlined in this book.

By reading this document, the readers agree that under no circumstances are the author responsible for any losses, direct or indirect, which are incurred as a result of the use of information contained within this document, including but not limited to errors, omissions or inaccuracies.

Thank you very much for reading this book.

Title: ChronoFallacy: Crushing Dreams of Time Travel
Subtitle: Why You'll Never Escape Yesterday and Tomorrow is Forever Out of Reach

Author: Blaze X. Maverick

Table of Contents

Introduction 6
Overview of the fascination with time travel in popular culture 6
The central thesis: Time travel, as commonly imagined, is inherently impossible 10
Setting the tone for exploring theoretical, philosophical, and scientific aspects 14

Chapter 1: Exploring Theoretical Constraints 18
Fundamental physics principles and their implications for time travel 18
The Novikov self-consistency principle and its limitations 22
Addressing the challenges posed by causality and the arrow of time 28
Highlighting theoretical models that point to the impossibility of time travel 34

Chapter 2: Philosophical Considerations 41
The grandfather paradox and its philosophical implications 41
Time travel's impact on concepts of free will and determinism 48
Other philosophical paradoxes associated with time travel 56
Examining how time travel challenges our understanding of the universe 62

Chapter 3: Scientific Challenges 68

Technological barriers to achieving time travel 68
Energy requirements and the impracticality of generating the necessary power 75
Time dilation and the difficulties associated with achieving the required speeds 82
Scientific arguments against the feasibility of time travel. 91

Chapter 4: Historical Impact 98
Chaos and disruptions in historical events if time travel were possible 98
Unintended consequences and the fragility of historical occurrences 106
Imagining scenarios of historical interference and their implications 114
Discussing the potential risks of altering the course of history 123

Chapter 5: Human Limitations 130
Biological constraints on humans attempting time travel 130
Impact on the human body and mind 137
Psychological challenges associated with time travel 143
Addressing the impracticality of human involvement in time-travel scenarios 150

Chapter 6: Alternative Perspectives 156
Dissenting opinions within the scientific and philosophical communities 156
Exploring unconventional theories challenging mainstream views 163

Speculative, non-standard perspectives on the nature of time 170
Examining the diversity of thought on the possibility of time travel 176
Conclusion 181
Summarizing key arguments against the possibility of time travel 181
Reinforcing the central thesis: Time travel, as commonly conceived, is not achievable 186
Encouraging readers to appreciate the imaginative aspect of time travel while recognizing its implausibility 192
Glossary 199
Potential References 201

Introduction
Overview of the fascination with time travel in popular culture

In the vast tapestry of human imagination, few concepts have captured the collective fascination as profoundly as the idea of time travel. The mere mention of these words conjures visions of futuristic machines, swirling wormholes, and the tantalizing prospect of altering the past or glimpsing into the future. From the hallowed halls of science fiction to the speculative corridors of philosophy, the allure of temporal manipulation has transcended generations, permeating popular culture in myriad forms.

The Cinematic Odyssey:

One of the primary conduits through which the enchantment of time travel has permeated society is the silver screen. Countless movies have thrust audiences into temporal odysseys, each narrative thread weaving a unique tale of temporal manipulation. Classics like "Back to the Future" ignited the imaginations of audiences, showcasing the potential for hilarity, drama, and unforeseen consequences when the fabric of time is tampered with. The relentless pursuit of the perfect time travel narrative has birthed iconic films, leaving an indelible mark on popular culture.

However, the cinematic portrayal of time travel is not confined to the comedic or the dramatic; it extends to the realms of mind-bending complexity and philosophical introspection. Films like "Primer" and "Interstellar" delve into the intricacies of theoretical physics, challenging audiences to grapple with concepts such as time dilation and the bending of spacetime. These cinematic forays not only entertain but also serve as conduits for introducing complex scientific theories to the public consciousness.

Literary Landscapes:

Beyond the visual medium, literature has been a fertile ground for the cultivation of time travel narratives. H.G. Wells, often hailed as the pioneer of time travel fiction, unleashed "The Time Machine" upon the world in 1895, laying the foundation for a literary genre that would blossom over the ensuing decades. Writers like Isaac Asimov, Ray Bradbury, and Kurt Vonnegut have woven intricate temporal tapestries, exploring the philosophical, ethical, and existential dimensions of traversing through time.

These literary excursions into time's enigmatic folds often serve as more than just entertainment; they are vehicles for exploring the human condition. Time travel narratives become a lens through which authors dissect societal norms, question the inevitability of destiny, and ponder the consequences of human agency over the temporal domain.

Time Travel in Television:

Television, with its episodic nature, has offered creators an expansive canvas to paint intricate time travel sagas. Series like "Doctor Who" have become cultural phenomena, captivating audiences with the adventures of a time-traveling alien. The small screen has witnessed a proliferation of temporal twists and paradoxes, from the mind-bending narratives of "Lost" to the speculative brilliance of "The Twilight Zone." Television not only reflects society's fascination with time travel but also shapes and evolves the discourse surrounding its possibilities.

Temporal Themes in Popular Music:

The rhythmic beats of popular music have also echoed with temporal motifs. Artists across genres have explored the theme of time travel, infusing their lyrics with the desire to rewind the clock or fast-forward into the unknown. Whether it's the poignant reflections of Jim Croce's "Time in a Bottle" or the futuristic fantasies of David Bowie's "Life on Mars," music serves as both a mirror and a catalyst for our collective obsession with temporality.

Conclusion of Overview:

The fascination with time travel in popular culture is a multifaceted phenomenon, weaving through the realms of cinema, literature, television, and music. It taps into our innate curiosity about the nature of time, the possibilities of altering our destinies, and the consequences of wielding such immense power. As we embark on this exploration, it becomes evident that our cultural fascination with time travel is not merely a transient trend but a timeless quest to unravel the mysteries of existence. In the chapters that follow, we shall dissect the illusions surrounding time travel, revealing the stark realities that defy the fantasies perpetuated by our cultural obsessions.

The central thesis: Time travel, as commonly imagined, is inherently impossible

As we embark on this journey into the heart of temporal mysteries, it is imperative to establish a foundational truth that forms the bedrock of our exploration: time travel, as commonly imagined, is inherently impossible. This bold assertion serves as our guiding principle, cutting through the fabric of popular culture's temporal fantasies and laying bare the inherent limitations imposed by the laws of physics, philosophy, and the very nature of time itself.

Theoretical Constraints:

At the nexus of our temporal odyssey lies the formidable realm of theoretical physics. Here, the laws that govern the cosmos intertwine with the elusive nature of time, presenting an intricate tapestry that resists the threads of temporal manipulation. Fundamental principles such as causality and the arrow of time stand as sentinels, guarding against the whims of temporal trespassers.

In the labyrinth of theoretical constraints, the Novikov self-consistency principle emerges as a beacon of limitation. This theoretical construct, born from the fertile mind of physicist Igor Novikov, posits that the universe conspires to prevent any actions that would create a paradox. In essence, it is a safeguard against the disruption of the space-time continuum, a mechanism that renders the very concept of altering the past a self-nullifying paradox.

Causality, the linchpin of temporal order, resists manipulation with an unyielding force. The notion that an effect can precede its cause, a staple of time travel fantasies, stands in direct contradiction to the fundamental principles that underpin our understanding of the universe.

Philosophical Considerations:

As we navigate the temporal labyrinth, philosophical paradoxes cast long shadows upon the landscape of possibility. The grandfather paradox, a perennial puzzle in the annals of temporal contemplation, challenges the very fabric of logical coherence. If one were to travel back in time and alter the course of familial events, the paradox arises: How could the time traveler exist to perform such an act if the altered events would prevent their own existence?

The philosophical implications extend beyond familial ties, delving into the bedrock of human agency. The concept of free will, a cornerstone of our understanding of existence, clashes with the deterministic underpinnings of time travel. If the past, present, and future are malleable, our choices become mere illusions, scripted by the cosmic ballet of temporal manipulations.

Scientific Challenges:

Turning our gaze towards the realm of empirical inquiry, we encounter insurmountable scientific challenges that bar the path to temporal manipulation. Technological barriers, the proverbial gates barring entry into the temporal frontier, loom large. The sheer energy requirements for bending spacetime, creating wormholes, or achieving relativistic speeds approach levels that defy our current understanding of physics.

The dream of a time machine, a vessel capable of traversing the corridors of time, collides with the harsh reality of energy constraints. Theoretical models that promise shortcuts through time demand quantities of energy that surpass the limits of our current technological capabilities.

Time dilation, a consequence of Einstein's theory of relativity, introduces another formidable hurdle. As one approaches the speed of light, time dilates, stretching and warping the very fabric of temporal reality. However, achieving the necessary speeds for meaningful time travel becomes an endeavor fraught with insurmountable challenges.

Scientific arguments against the feasibility of time travel stand as a formidable bastion against the tide of popular fantasy. The laws of thermodynamics, particularly the second law, cast doubt upon the reversibility of certain temporal processes, adding another layer of complexity to the temporal puzzle.

Conclusion of the Central Thesis:

In the crucible of theoretical constraints, philosophical paradoxes, and scientific challenges, the central thesis crystallizes: time travel, as commonly imagined, is inherently impossible. As we navigate the chapters that follow, we will dismantle the illusions perpetuated by popular culture, exposing the stark realities that defy the temporal fantasies that have captured the collective imagination. Our journey is one of revelation, uncovering the harsh truths that lay hidden beneath the allure of time travel.

Setting the tone for exploring theoretical, philosophical, and scientific aspects

As we stand at the threshold of our temporal expedition, the air is charged with the electricity of anticipation. The quest before us is no mere jaunt through the annals of fantasy; it is an intellectual odyssey, a journey into the heart of theoretical abstractions, philosophical ponderings, and scientific enigma. In the following passages, we shall unfurl the layers of time like a cosmic scroll, revealing the intricacies that entwine the very fabric of existence.

Theoretical Dance of Possibility:

Our journey commences in the ethereal realm of theoretical physics, where the laws that govern the cosmos unfold in a cosmic ballet. Theories, as ephemeral as stardust, shimmer with potentialities and paradoxes. Here, time is not a linear procession but a tapestry, woven with threads of relativity and quantum mechanics.

Albert Einstein, the architect of the theory of relativity, reshaped our understanding of time and space. In the dazzling equations of his theories, time emerges not as an absolute constant but as a dynamic, mutable force. The warp and weft of spacetime create the stage upon which the cosmic drama unfolds, beckoning us to unravel the mysteries that lie within.

Quantum mechanics, the quantum dance of particles and probabilities, introduces a layer of uncertainty to the temporal narrative. The very act of observation alters the observed, challenging the notion of a deterministic universe. As we navigate the quantum labyrinth, the contours of possibility blur, inviting us to question the very nature of causality.

Philosophical Echoes in the Halls of Time:

With theoretical threads in hand, we step into the hallowed halls of philosophy, where the echoes of temporal contemplation resonate through the ages. The very essence of time becomes a philosophical quandary, a puzzle that eludes easy categorization. Is time an absolute truth, an immutable river flowing from past to future, or is it a subjective illusion, a construct of human perception?

Theories of time within philosophy span the spectrum from eternalism to presentism. Eternalism posits that past, present, and future coexist, an unchanging tableau where all moments persist. Presentism, on the other hand, asserts the reality only of the present, relegating past and future to the realms of memory and anticipation.

Temporal paradoxes, the philosophical conundrums that arise from contemplating time travel, cast long shadows. The grandfather paradox, a perennial puzzle, challenges the logical coherence of altering the past. Free will, a cornerstone of philosophical discourse, encounters turbulence when faced with the determinism inherent in certain time travel scenarios.

Scientific Alchemy of Temporal Reality:

Having traversed the theoretical and philosophical landscapes, we descend into the crucible of scientific inquiry. Here, the alchemy of empirical investigation transmutes the abstract into the tangible, the speculative into the measurable. Our quest for temporal understanding now wades into the waters of concrete experimentation and observation.

Technological marvels become our vessels of exploration. The Large Hadron Collider, a colossal particle accelerator, peels back the layers of subatomic reality, probing the very foundations of existence. While not a time machine in the classical sense, the experiments conducted within its colossal rings offer glimpses into the subtleties of time's dance.

As we navigate the realm of quantum entanglement, the phenomenon where particles share a mysterious connection regardless of distance, the very nature of time's arrow comes into question. Could entanglement be the ethereal link that transcends temporal boundaries?

The practical challenges of time travel materialize in the harsh light of scientific scrutiny. The energy requirements for bending spacetime or creating wormholes approach levels that defy our current technological capabilities. Theoretical models, while elegant in their abstraction, demand technological feats that stand on the precipice of the possible.

Synthesis of Theoretical, Philosophical, and Scientific Strands:

In the harmonious convergence of theoretical abstraction, philosophical contemplation, and scientific scrutiny, we find ourselves poised at the intersection of the conceivable and the inconceivable. Our journey is one of synthesis, weaving together the threads of theory, philosophy, and science into a tapestry that seeks to unravel the secrets of time.

As we delve into the chapters that follow, each facet of our exploration will be illuminated, dissected, and laid bare. The theoretical, the philosophical, and the scientific will coalesce, offering a panoramic view of the complexities that shroud time travel in an enigmatic veil. Prepare, dear reader, for an odyssey that transcends the boundaries of imagination and ventures into the uncharted territories of temporal reality.

Chapter 1: Exploring Theoretical Constraints
Fundamental physics principles and their implications for time travel

In the cosmic overture of theoretical physics, the maestro's baton is held by none other than Albert Einstein and his magnum opus, the theory of relativity. At the heart of this symphony lies the realization that time is not an immutable river but a dynamic current, flowing and bending in response to the gravitational forces exerted by massive celestial bodies.

The first movement, known as special relativity, redefined our understanding of time and space. Einstein's famous equation, $E=mc^2$, unveiled the interconnectedness of energy and mass, shattering the classical distinctions between the two. As particles approach the speed of light, time dilates, stretching and warping the very fabric of reality.

In the second movement, general relativity, gravity emerges as the sculptor of spacetime. Massive objects create gravitational wells, causing time to flow at different rates in their proximity. This gravitational time dilation, a consequence of general relativity, introduces a crucial nuance to our temporal journey.

Temporal Fabric and Spacetime Continuum:

As we delve deeper into the theoretical underpinnings of time travel, the concept of spacetime emerges as a crucial tapestry that interweaves the dimensions of space and time into a seamless continuum. In this four-dimensional fabric, events are not isolated occurrences but interconnected nodes in the grand ballet of existence.

Einstein's field equations, the mathematical scaffolding of general relativity, describe how matter and energy influence the curvature of spacetime. Wormholes, hypothetical tunnels through spacetime, become tantalizing possibilities. If we could manipulate these cosmic conduits, a shortcut through the vast distances of the universe might be achievable.

However, the theoretical construction of wormholes is not without its challenges. Stabilizing these tunnels against the tidal forces that threaten to collapse them requires exotic matter with negative energy density, a substance that exists more in the realm of theory than empirical observation.

Causality and the Arrow of Time:

As we navigate the temporal currents, the fundamental principle of causality stands as a sentinel, guarding against the whims of temporal trespassers. Causality dictates that an event cannot precede its cause, establishing a sequential order that governs the unfolding of reality.

The arrow of time, an intrinsic property of the universe, points in the direction of increasing entropy. Events progress from ordered states to disordered states, a one-way journey that defines the irreversibility of time. This inherent asymmetry clashes with the symmetrical expectations of many time travel scenarios.

Temporal paradoxes, the narrative disruptions that arise from violating causality, cast long shadows over the landscape of possibility. The grandfather paradox, where a time traveler alters the past in a way that prevents their own existence, challenges the logical coherence of time travel narratives.

Quantum Mechanics and the Uncertainty Principle:

As we journey deeper into the quantum realm, the deterministic certainties of classical physics give way to the probabilistic dance of quantum mechanics. Here, particles exist in a state of uncertainty, their properties defined by probability distributions rather than exact values.

The Heisenberg Uncertainty Principle, a foundational concept in quantum mechanics, asserts that the more precisely we know the position of a particle, the less precisely we can know its momentum, and vice versa. This inherent uncertainty introduces a degree of fuzziness into the fabric of reality, challenging the notion of a deterministic universe.

Quantum entanglement, the mysterious phenomenon where particles become linked in ways that defy classical intuitions, raises questions about the nature of causality itself. If particles can instantaneously influence each other's states regardless of distance, the conventional boundaries of cause and effect become blurred.

Temporal Loopholes and Cosmic Quirks:

In our exploration of fundamental physics principles, we encounter tantalizing possibilities that seem to defy the conventional constraints of time. Theoretical constructs such as closed timelike curves, paths through spacetime that loop back on themselves, invite speculation about potential temporal shortcuts.

However, the existence of closed timelike curves raises profound questions about consistency and paradoxes. The Novikov self-consistency principle, an elegant theoretical construct, posits that the universe conspires to prevent actions that would create paradoxes. In the realm of closed timelike curves, this principle becomes a safeguard against the disruption of the temporal continuum.

As we stand at the intersection of theoretical constraints and speculative possibilities, the cosmic symphony of relativity, the fabric of spacetime, the principles of causality, and the quirks of quantum mechanics beckon us further into the depths of temporal exploration. In the chapters that follow, each note of this cosmic composition will be dissected, scrutinized, and laid bare, revealing the intricacies and limitations that bind time within the embrace of the cosmic symphony.

The Novikov self-consistency principle and its limitations

In the labyrinth of theoretical constraints that govern time travel, one of the guiding lights is the Novikov self-consistency principle. Conceived by Russian physicist Igor Novikov, this principle seeks to reconcile the paradoxes that arise from temporal manipulations by proposing a stringent framework of self-consistency. As we unravel the threads of this enigma, we delve into a theoretical landscape where the past, present, and future coalesce into a harmonious tapestry.

Foundations of the Novikov Self-Consistency Principle:

At its core, the Novikov self-consistency principle asserts that any action or event that an observer might take in the past must be inherently consistent with the existing state of affairs. In simpler terms, the principle acts as a cosmic safeguard against the creation of paradoxes through time travel. If an event appears to be paradoxical or contradictory, the principle stipulates that it cannot occur.

Consider, for instance, a time traveler attempting to alter the past in a way that would prevent their own existence—a classic temporal paradox known as the grandfather paradox. According to the Novikov self-consistency principle, any action taken by the time traveler would be subtly influenced by the existing state of affairs, ensuring that the outcome remains consistent with the observer's past experiences.

Temporal Judo: Navigating the Paradoxical Landscape:

To comprehend the implications of the Novikov self-consistency principle, envision a temporal judo where attempts to disrupt the natural order are met with counterforces that redirect the flow of events. Novikov's theoretical framework proposes that the very fabric of spacetime resists paradoxical incursions, guiding the outcome of temporal interventions toward a self-consistent resolution.

In the context of the grandfather paradox, the principle might orchestrate a sequence of events that prevents the time traveler from altering the past in a way that negates their own existence. The universe, under the guiding hand of self-consistency, becomes a cosmic choreographer, ensuring that the temporal ballet adheres to the predefined steps.

The Cosmic Hand of Determinism:

Implicit in the Novikov self-consistency principle is a certain degree of determinism—a philosophical stance that asserts the inevitability of events based on existing conditions. If the past, present, and future are intertwined in a seamless continuum, then the choices and actions of individuals become intrinsically bound by the cosmic script.

This deterministic aspect introduces a layer of philosophical complexity to the temporal journey. Free will, a cherished concept that underpins our sense of agency and choice, encounters a formidable foe in the form of self-consistency. If every action is subtly influenced by the existing state of affairs, the illusion of free will becomes entangled in the cosmic dance of determinism.

Temporal Interactions: The Dance of Quantum Probabilities:

As we navigate the terrain of quantum mechanics and its implications for time travel, the Novikov self-consistency principle casts its shadow even into the probabilistic realms of quantum interactions. The delicate dance of particles, governed by uncertainty and probability, finds itself constrained by the cosmic imperative of self-consistency.

Quantum entanglement, the phenomenon where particles become correlated in ways that defy classical intuitions, introduces a level of intricacy to the self-consistency framework. The choices made by observers in the present, influencing the states of entangled particles, must align with the predetermined outcomes dictated by the Novikov principle.

In the quantum theater, the principle acts as a subtle orchestrator, guiding the probabilities of events to ensure that the fabric of spacetime remains untangled and consistent. The entangled particles, seemingly engaged in a cosmic conversation, follow a script that harmonizes with the observer's past experiences.

Limitations of the Novikov Self-Consistency Principle:

While the Novikov self-consistency principle provides an elegant solution to the potential paradoxes of time travel, it is not without its limitations. The very nature of these limitations adds nuance to our understanding of the principle and introduces intriguing questions about the broader scope of temporal exploration.

One limitation lies in the assumption of a single, self-consistent timeline. The principle operates on the premise that the universe converges on a singular path, guiding events toward a consistent resolution. However, some theories posit the existence of multiple timelines or parallel universes, each branching off with every temporal intervention.

The concept of parallel timelines challenges the strict determinism implied by the Novikov self-consistency principle. If every action subtly influences the existing state of affairs, the principle must contend with the divergent outcomes that arise in a multiverse scenario. The elegant choreography of events becomes a complex tapestry of possibilities, each strand weaving its own narrative.

Furthermore, the principle assumes an observer-centric perspective, anchoring self-consistency to the experiences and actions of a particular individual. This anthropocentric bias raises questions about the universality of the principle. If time travel were achievable, would the actions of different observers converge on a consistent narrative, or would divergent timelines emerge based on individual perspectives?

The Novikov self-consistency principle also grapples with the implications of closed timelike curves—hypothetical paths through spacetime that loop back on themselves. While the principle seeks to prevent paradoxes, the intricacies of closed timelike curves introduce challenges that are not fully resolved. The potential for causal loops, where events perpetually influence each other without clear initiation, adds a layer of complexity to the self-consistency framework.

In the face of these limitations, the Novikov self-consistency principle remains a powerful theoretical construct that shapes our understanding of time travel. Its elegant solution to the paradoxes of temporal manipulation invites further contemplation, challenging us to explore the intricate interplay between determinism, probability, and the inherent constraints of self-consistency.

Conclusion: The Cosmic Tapestry of Self-Consistent Realities:

As we emerge from the theoretical labyrinth of the Novikov self-consistency principle and its limitations, the tapestry of self-consistent realities unfurls before us. The principle, with its deterministic underpinnings and subtle orchestration of temporal events, offers a glimpse into the potential mechanisms that may govern the cosmic dance of time.

Yet, as we grapple with the intricacies and uncertainties introduced by quantum mechanics, the possibility of parallel timelines, and the challenges posed by closed timelike curves, the limitations of the principle become apparent. The cosmic tapestry, woven with threads of self-consistency, may conceal hidden patterns and divergent narratives that elude our current understanding.

In the chapters that follow, we will continue to dissect the theoretical constraints that shape our perception of time travel. Each layer peeled back reveals new complexities, inviting us to explore the frontiers of temporal exploration with a nuanced understanding of the enigmatic principles that govern the cosmic symphony of self-consistent realities.

Addressing the challenges posed by causality and the arrow of time

As we embark on the exploration of theoretical constraints in the realm of time travel, the principle of causality emerges as a formidable guardian of temporal order. Causality, the concept that an event cannot precede its cause, establishes a fundamental framework for the unfolding of reality. In this chapter, we delve into the intricacies of causality, unraveling its threads to understand the challenges it poses to the very fabric of time.

Causality as the Temporal Sentinel:

At the heart of our temporal journey lies the principle of causality, an intrepid sentinel that guards against the whims of temporal trespassers. Causality dictates a sequential order of events, where the past influences the present, and the present shapes the future. This arrow of causality, pointing inexorably from cause to effect, establishes a temporal tapestry that weaves through the cosmic fabric.

Consider a simple act, such as knocking over a domino. The falling domino becomes the cause, initiating a chain reaction that unfolds in a predetermined sequence. Causality dictates that the falling domino cannot be the effect of a subsequent action; it is the instigator, the temporal architect of the unfolding events.

In the realm of time travel, the challenge becomes apparent. If one were to traverse the corridors of time and alter the past, the established order of cause and effect would be disrupted. The familiar narrative of events, each influencing the next in a coherent sequence, faces the prospect of unraveling into chaos.

Temporal Entanglement: Causality and Quantum Mechanics:

As we delve into the quantum realm, the principles of causality encounter the nuanced dance of quantum mechanics. In the probabilistic landscape of subatomic particles, the deterministic certainties of classical causality give way to a realm of uncertainty and probability.

The Heisenberg Uncertainty Principle, a cornerstone of quantum mechanics, introduces an inherent fuzziness into the fabric of causality. The precise measurement of a particle's position disrupts our ability to know its momentum with certainty, and vice versa. The deterministic predictability of classical causality meets the indeterminacy of quantum uncertainty, challenging our intuitive understanding of cause and effect.

Quantum entanglement, the mysterious phenomenon where particles become correlated in ways that defy classical intuitions, adds another layer to the entanglement of causality. If the state of one entangled particle is influenced instantaneously by the measurement of its entangled partner, the linear flow of cause and effect becomes entwined in a non-local dance that transcends the constraints of classical causality.

Arrow of Time: The Inevitability of Entropy:

The arrow of time, an intrinsic property of the universe, complements the principle of causality by establishing a unidirectional flow of events. This temporal asymmetry, defined by the increase of entropy, dictates that events progress from ordered states to disordered states. The past, characterized by lower entropy and higher order, stands in stark contrast to the future, where entropy increases, leading to greater disorder.

Entropy, a measure of the disorder or randomness in a system, becomes a cosmic clock that aligns with the arrow of time. As we traverse the temporal landscape, the challenge becomes evident: altering the past in a way that contradicts the arrow of time disrupts the established narrative of increasing entropy.

Consider a scenario where a shattered glass spontaneously reassembles itself—a reversal of the natural progression from order to disorder. Such an event, while possible in the realm of imagination, clashes with the inexorable march of the arrow of time. The constraints imposed by entropy introduce challenges to the feasibility of time travel scenarios that involve significant alterations to the established order of events.

Temporal Trespass: Challenges to Causality in Time Travel Narratives:

In the annals of time travel fiction, narratives often grapple with the challenges posed by causality. The grandfather paradox, a perennial puzzle, embodies the temporal trespass that disrupts the established order of cause and effect. If one were to travel back in time and alter a crucial event, the consequences could lead to a cascade of changes that ultimately prevent the time traveler's own existence—a paradox that challenges the logical coherence of temporal narratives.

Time loops, another common trope in time travel stories, introduce circular causality. Events perpetually influence each other in a closed loop, creating a temporal circuit where cause and effect become intertwined in an eternal dance. While these narrative constructs captivate the imagination, they highlight the challenges of maintaining a coherent causal sequence in the face of temporal manipulations.

Resolving Causality Conundrums: Theoretical Approaches:

In the realm of theoretical physics, several approaches seek to address the causality conundrums posed by time travel scenarios. The Novikov self-consistency principle, as discussed in the previous section, proposes a framework where the universe conspires to prevent actions that would create paradoxes. This self-regulating mechanism guides temporal interventions toward outcomes that remain consistent with the observer's past experiences.

Another theoretical approach involves the notion of parallel timelines or branching universes. If every temporal intervention leads to the creation of a divergent timeline, the challenges posed by causality in altering the established order become less pronounced. Each timeline unfolds independently, preserving the causal sequence within its own narrative arc.

Closed timelike curves, hypothetical paths through spacetime that loop back on themselves, introduce complexities to the causality puzzle. The resolution of causality challenges in the presence of closed timelike curves remains an active area of theoretical exploration, with some models suggesting that consistent outcomes may still be possible within the confines of self-consistency.

Philosophical Implications: Causality and Free Will:

As we navigate the challenges posed by causality and the arrow of time, philosophical implications come to the fore. The concept of free will, a cornerstone of human agency, encounters turbulence in the face of deterministic constraints. If causality and the arrow of time conspire to shape events along a predetermined path, the illusion of free will becomes entangled in the cosmic dance of temporal order.

Determinism, the philosophical stance that all events are predetermined by existing conditions, challenges the notion of autonomous choice. If every action is a consequence of preceding events, the narrative of free will becomes a mirage, veiled by the deterministic forces that govern the unfolding of reality.

However, the philosophical landscape is nuanced. Some argue that the constraints imposed by causality and the arrow of time do not negate the concept of free will but shape its contours. The choices we make, while influenced by the past and constrained by the direction of time, still carry a sense of agency and responsibility.

Conclusion: Navigating the Temporal Currents:

As we navigate the currents of causality and grapple with the challenges posed by the arrow of time, the temporal landscape unfolds before us as a complex tapestry. Causality, the guardian of temporal order, and the arrow of time, the cosmic clock of entropy, shape the narrative of our existence.

In the chapters that follow, we will continue to unravel the theoretical constraints that define the contours of time travel. Each thread pulled reveals new intricacies, inviting us to explore the frontiers of temporal manipulation with a nuanced understanding of the challenges posed by causality and the unidirectional flow of time. The temporal currents, while formidable, beckon us to navigate the waters of possibility and uncover the mysteries that lie beneath the surface of temporal exploration.

Highlighting theoretical models that point to the impossibility of time travel

As we plunge into the depths of theoretical constraints surrounding time travel, an array of models emerges, each casting a skeptical shadow over the possibility of temporal manipulation. In this chapter, we will examine the theoretical frameworks that paint time travel as an elusive mirage, perpetually just out of reach due to the inherent complexities and contradictions woven into the fabric of reality.

Time Travel and the Laws of Thermodynamics:

A foundational pillar of theoretical physics, the laws of thermodynamics, casts doubt on the feasibility of time travel scenarios that involve significant alterations to the established order of events. The second law of thermodynamics, often summarized as the increase of entropy in a closed system, posits that natural processes tend to move towards states of greater disorder.

The implications of the second law become apparent when contemplating time travel scenarios that defy the arrow of time. If one were to travel back and prevent a significant event from occurring, the entropy of the universe would seemingly decrease, violating the natural progression towards greater disorder. The concept of a shattered glass spontaneously reassembling itself, in defiance of entropy, becomes a challenging puzzle for proponents of time travel.

Theoretical models grounded in thermodynamics suggest that the very nature of temporal manipulation may be at odds with the fundamental principles that govern the behavior of matter and energy. The impossibility of circumventing the relentless march of entropy stands as a formidable barrier to the realization of time travel as commonly imagined.

Chronology Protection Conjecture: A Cosmic Safeguard:

Proposed by physicist Stephen Hawking, the Chronology Protection Conjecture adds another layer of skepticism to the prospect of time travel. Hawking postulated that the laws of physics inherently conspire to prevent the creation of closed timelike curves—hypothetical paths through spacetime that loop back on themselves and could potentially enable time travel.

The conjecture suggests that as soon as a potential time loop or closed timelike curve begins to form, the laws of physics intervene to prevent its completion. Quantum fluctuations, vacuum fluctuations, or any other exotic phenomena would disrupt the emergence of a closed timelike curve, ensuring that the temporal continuity of the universe remains intact.

In essence, the Chronology Protection Conjecture proposes a cosmic safeguard against the disruption of causality and the creation of paradoxes through time travel. If the laws of physics actively resist the formation of closed timelike curves, the very pathways that could facilitate time travel are rendered elusive and unattainable.

Quantum Mechanics and the Uncertainty Principle:

Delving deeper into the realm of quantum mechanics, the Heisenberg Uncertainty Principle introduces a level of uncertainty that challenges the deterministic expectations often associated with time travel scenarios. The principle asserts that the more precisely we know the position of a particle, the less precisely we can know its momentum, and vice versa.

In the context of time travel, the uncertainty principle introduces a fundamental fuzziness into the fabric of reality. The precise determination of the initial conditions required for temporal interventions becomes an elusive goal. The very act of measuring and determining the necessary parameters introduces uncertainties that cascade through the temporal landscape.

Quantum mechanics, with its probabilistic nature, raises questions about the predictability and control necessary for achieving precise temporal manipulations. The uncertainties embedded in quantum phenomena, when scaled up to the macroscopic level of time travel scenarios, create formidable challenges that cast doubt on the feasibility of manipulating time with precision.

Grandfather Paradox: An Intricate Web of Contradictions:

At the heart of time travel skepticism lies the Grandfather Paradox, a conceptual tangle that challenges the logical coherence of altering the past. If one were to travel back in time and prevent their grandfather from meeting their grandmother, the paradox unfolds: the time traveler's existence becomes a contradiction, a loop that defies the linear narrative of cause and effect.

Theoretical models that emphasize the intricacies of the Grandfather Paradox suggest that the mere possibility of such a contradiction may signal the implausibility of time travel as commonly imagined. The paradox creates a web of contradictions and self-reference that appears to resist resolution within the framework of consistent and coherent temporal manipulation.

Models that explore the Grandfather Paradox often highlight the potential for logical inconsistencies and paradoxical loops that emerge when attempting to alter the past. Whether through alternative timelines or self-consistency principles, theoretical frameworks often point to the complexity and instability introduced by the very notion of retroactively changing historical events.

Wormholes and the Energy Conundrum:

Theoretical constructs like wormholes, often envisioned as cosmic shortcuts through spacetime, face a formidable challenge grounded in the energy requirements necessary for their creation and stabilization. While the concept of a traversable wormhole captures the imagination, the practicalities of generating and sustaining such exotic structures pose significant hurdles.

The energy required to keep a wormhole stable, according to theoretical models, approaches levels that defy current technological capabilities and known physical limits. Exotic matter with negative energy density, a hypothetical substance that counters the gravitational forces working to collapse the wormhole, remains elusive and unobserved.

Theoretical models that address the energy conundrum associated with wormholes emphasize the immense challenges posed by the practicalities of time travel. Theoretical constructs may suggest the existence of traversable wormholes, but the realization of such cosmic gateways appears to be beyond the reach of current scientific understanding and technological prowess.

String Theory and Multiverse Hypotheses:

String theory, an ambitious theoretical framework seeking to unify the fundamental forces of nature, introduces additional layers of complexity to the question of time travel. In the context of string theory, the very nature of spacetime and the dimensions that define reality become subject to intricate symphonies of vibrating strings.

Some string theory models suggest the existence of multiple dimensions and parallel universes— a multiverse. Within this multiverse framework, the challenges and impossibilities associated with time travel may vary from one dimension to another, introducing a level of unpredictability and variability that challenges the notion of a universally attainable time travel technology.

Theoretical models within string theory propose that the properties of our universe, including the potential for time travel, are intricately linked to the specific parameters and conditions within a particular dimension. As we explore the vast landscape of potential universes within the multiverse, the question of whether time travel is universally possible or contingent on specific cosmic conditions becomes a tantalizing puzzle.

Conclusion: The Elusive Frontier of Temporal Manipulation:

In the labyrinth of theoretical constraints surrounding time travel, the models explored in this chapter paint a compelling narrative of skepticism and implausibility. The laws of thermodynamics, the Chronology Protection Conjecture, the uncertainties of quantum mechanics, the enigma of the Grandfather Paradox, the energy challenges of wormholes, and the intricate symphonies of string theory collectively contribute to a theoretical landscape where time travel appears to be an elusive frontier.

As we navigate the theoretical intricacies and confront the inherent challenges woven into the fabric of reality, the prospect of manipulating time with the ease often depicted in fiction becomes a mirage on the horizon. The elusive nature of time travel beckons us to consider the limitations imposed by the very principles that govern the cosmos.

In the chapters that follow, we will continue our exploration, dissecting additional theoretical frameworks and delving into the broader implications of the impossibility of time travel. Each layer peeled back reveals new nuances and complexities, inviting us to appreciate the profound intricacies that define the frontier between imagination and the immutable laws of the universe.

Chapter 2: Philosophical Considerations
The grandfather paradox and its philosophical implications

In the annals of time travel contemplation, the Grandfather Paradox stands as a seminal puzzle that tests the logical coherence of altering the past. The paradox, often encapsulated in a simple question—what if one were to travel back in time and prevent their grandfather from meeting their grandmother?—unleashes a cascade of contradictions that weave an intricate narrative of temporal entanglement.

Temporal Incursion and Ancestral Ripples:

At the heart of the Grandfather Paradox lies the act of temporal incursion—a journey into the past with the intention of altering a crucial event. In this case, the intervention centers around preventing the meeting of the time traveler's grandfather and grandmother, a seemingly innocuous act with profound consequences.

Consider the hypothetical time traveler, armed with the knowledge of their familial lineage, embarking on a quest to alter the course of history. The act of preventing the initial encounter between their grandparents introduces ripples through the fabric of time, disrupting the established narrative of familial lineage and altering the circumstances that led to their own existence.

As the temporal incursion unfolds, a web of contradictions emerges. If the time traveler succeeds in preventing the meeting, the future that led to their birth unravels. Yet, if the meeting is prevented, the time traveler's existence becomes a paradox—a contradiction that challenges the very foundations of cause and effect.

Philosophical Implications: The Butterfly Effect and Determinism:

The Grandfather Paradox delves into the heart of philosophical considerations surrounding causality and determinism. The scenario introduces a variant of the Butterfly Effect—a concept in chaos theory suggesting that small changes in initial conditions can lead to vastly different outcomes. In this case, the seemingly minor act of preventing a chance meeting between two individuals sets off a chain reaction with far-reaching consequences.

The philosophical implications become apparent when examining the interplay between determinism and free will. Determinism, the philosophical stance that all events are predetermined by existing conditions, encounters turbulence when confronted with the prospect of retroactive changes to the past. If the past can be altered, the deterministic tapestry of cause and effect becomes malleable, challenging the notion of a predetermined and predictable universe.

Free will, entangled in the paradoxical narrative, faces a conundrum. The time traveler's act of altering the past may be perceived as an exercise of free will—an autonomous choice that reshapes the course of history. However, if the altered past leads to the time traveler's own non-existence, the illusion of free will clashes with the deterministic forces that govern the consequences of temporal interventions.

Parallel Timelines and Multiverse Hypotheses:

Philosophical considerations surrounding the Grandfather Paradox often intersect with theoretical models proposing the existence of parallel timelines or branching universes within a multiverse framework. These models offer potential resolutions to the paradox by suggesting that the act of altering the past creates a divergence—a branching path that leads to an alternative timeline.

In this interpretation, the time traveler's actions do not erase their existence but rather spawn a parallel reality where the altered past unfolds independently. The multiverse hypothesis introduces a level of variability that mitigates the paradoxical contradictions inherent in the linear timeline of a single universe.

The philosophical implications of parallel timelines raise questions about the nature of identity and the self. If the time traveler's actions lead to the creation of an alternative timeline, does the version of themselves in that timeline possess a distinct identity and consciousness? The philosophical exploration extends beyond the consequences of temporal interventions to the very essence of personal identity within a multiversal framework.

Temporal Logic and Self-Consistency:

The Grandfather Paradox prompts a deeper exploration of temporal logic and the principles that govern self-consistency. The Novikov self-consistency principle, discussed earlier in the exploration of theoretical constraints, offers a philosophical lens through which to view the paradox. According to this principle, the universe conspires to prevent actions that would create paradoxes, guiding the outcomes of temporal interventions toward self-consistent resolutions.

In the context of the Grandfather Paradox, the self-consistency principle suggests that the time traveler's attempts to alter the past would be subtly influenced by the existing state of affairs. The universe, in its cosmic choreography, may orchestrate events that prevent the prevention—maintaining a self-consistent narrative where the time traveler's existence remains intact.

Philosophically, the self-consistency principle raises profound questions about the nature of agency and the boundaries of human intervention. If the universe actively resists paradoxical incursions, the exercise of free will becomes entangled in a cosmic dance where the consequences of temporal actions align with the existing state of affairs. The philosophical implications extend beyond the individual act of time travel to broader questions about the limits of human agency within the tapestry of time.

Temporal Morality: The Ethics of Altering History:

As we grapple with the philosophical implications of the Grandfather Paradox, ethical considerations come to the forefront. The act of altering the past raises profound questions about the responsibility and consequences of temporal interventions. If one possesses the ability to reshape history, what ethical considerations should guide their actions?

The ethical dimensions of time travel delve into the potential impacts on individuals and societies. The alteration of historical events may lead to unintended consequences, introducing chaos and disruptions that ripple through the fabric of time. The philosophical exploration extends to questions of accountability and the moral implications of wielding temporal power.

Moreover, the Grandfather Paradox prompts reflection on the ethical implications of erasing or preventing the existence of individuals. The very act of altering the past to negate the birth of certain individuals raises questions about the value of individual lives and the ethical boundaries of temporal interventions.

Existential Considerations: The Nature of Being and Non-Being:

The Grandfather Paradox invites contemplation on existential questions regarding the nature of being and non-being. The paradox, at its core, challenges the continuity of individual existence across temporal dimensions. If the altered past leads to the non-existence of the time traveler, the philosophical exploration extends to questions about the transient and contingent nature of individual identity.

Philosophically, the paradox prompts consideration of the nature of existence beyond the constraints of linear time. Does non-existence in a particular timeline imply an absolute cessation of being, or does it suggest a transition to a state beyond the scope of temporal logic? The exploration delves into the philosophical nuances of existence, consciousness, and the intricate interplay between individual identity and the temporal landscape.

Conclusion: Navigating the Paradoxical Landscape:

In the tapestry of time travel contemplation, the Grandfather Paradox emerges as a focal point for philosophical inquiry. The complexities and contradictions woven into the narrative of altering the past beckon us to navigate the paradoxical landscape with a nuanced understanding of causality, determinism, and the ethical dimensions of temporal interventions.

As we delve into the philosophical implications of the Grandfather Paradox, the exploration extends beyond the theoretical constraints and enters the realms of identity, morality, and existential considerations. The paradox serves as a philosophical crucible, inviting us to confront the profound questions that arise when contemplating the malleability of time.

In the chapters that follow, we will continue our philosophical journey, dissecting additional considerations and delving into the broader implications of time travel on the human experience. Each layer peeled back reveals new facets of the paradoxical landscape, inviting us to explore the frontiers of philosophical inquiry within the realms of temporal manipulation.

Time travel's impact on concepts of free will and determinism

As we navigate the intricate landscape of time travel, the profound interplay between concepts of free will and determinism emerges as a central philosophical undercurrent. The ability to journey through time, alter the course of events, and potentially reshape the future introduces complexities that resonate with age-old debates about the nature of human agency and the predetermining forces that govern the universe.

Free Will: The Loom of Autonomy:

At the heart of human experience lies the concept of free will—a tapestry of autonomy woven into the fabric of consciousness. Free will embodies the idea that individuals possess the capacity to make choices independent of deterministic constraints. It is the essence of agency, the ability to shape one's destiny through a series of conscious decisions.

Temporal manipulation, with its potential to alter the past and influence the future, casts a spotlight on the nature of free will. If individuals can traverse temporal landscapes and actively intervene in historical events, the exercise of free will becomes entangled in a cosmic dance where the choices made today may ripple through time, shaping the unfolding narrative of existence.

The philosophical exploration of free will within the context of time travel raises profound questions about the boundaries of human agency. Does the ability to alter the past imply an extension of free will beyond the immediate present? If one can rewrite the pages of history, the temporal canvas becomes an expansive realm where choices reverberate through the corridors of time.

Determinism: The Threads of Cosmic Symmetry:

In the cosmic tapestry of determinism, the trajectory of events unfolds with the inevitability of woven threads. Determinism posits that every state of the universe, including human actions, is predetermined by preceding conditions. The past, present, and future exist as interconnected strands, each influencing the other in a seamless dance of causality.

Temporal manipulation, when viewed through the lens of determinism, introduces a paradox. If the course of events is predetermined, the act of altering the past may appear as a predetermined link in the chain of causation. The very notion of free will, the capacity for autonomous choice, collides with the deterministic forces that govern the unfolding narrative of reality.

Philosophically, determinism prompts reflection on the nature of choice and causation within the temporal landscape. If the future is intricately connected to the past, the choices made today may be perceived as predetermined outcomes of preceding conditions. The illusion of autonomy becomes entangled in the deterministic threads that weave the tapestry of time.

Temporal Entanglement: Free Will within Deterministic Boundaries:

The interplay between free will and determinism within the context of time travel creates a tapestry of temporal entanglement. As individuals navigate the corridors of time, the choices they make become threads woven into the fabric of a predetermined universe. The exercise of free will, while apparent on the surface, encounters the deterministic constraints that govern the continuity of causation.

Consider a time traveler faced with a crucial decision—whether to alter a historical event or allow it to unfold according to its predetermined course. The act of choice, seemingly an expression of free will, becomes a temporal entanglement where the decision made may be intricately linked to the predetermined state of the universe.

Philosophically, this entanglement prompts inquiry into the nature of choice within the constraints of determinism. Can free will exist within a universe where the past, present, and future are interconnected by the unbroken threads of causation? The exploration extends beyond the immediate consequences of temporal interventions to broader questions about the boundaries of human agency within the deterministic confines of the cosmic dance.

Temporal Divergence: Parallel Realities and Alternative Paths:

The concept of parallel timelines or branching universes within a multiverse framework introduces a layer of complexity to the philosophical exploration of free will and determinism. If each temporal intervention leads to the creation of an alternative reality, the philosophical implications extend to questions about the nature of choice across divergent paths.

In this interpretation, the exercise of free will may transcend the deterministic boundaries of a single timeline. Each decision, each choice made by individuals navigating the temporal landscape, creates a divergence—a branching path where the consequences unfold independently of the deterministic threads governing the original timeline.

Philosophically, the consideration of parallel realities prompts reflection on the nature of choice across divergent timelines. Does the exercise of free will become a multi-dimensional phenomenon, extending across the tapestry of alternative paths? The exploration navigates the intricacies of identity and agency within the multiversal framework, inviting contemplation on the expansive nature of choice beyond the confines of a singular deterministic narrative.

Temporal Paradoxes: Navigating the Labyrinth of Self-Consistency:

Temporal paradoxes, such as the Grandfather Paradox, inject a dose of complexity into the philosophical inquiry of free will and determinism. The self-consistency principle, proposed to address paradoxes arising from time travel, posits that the universe actively prevents actions that would create inconsistencies.

Philosophically, this principle introduces a layer of determinism within the context of time travel. If the universe guides temporal interventions toward self-consistent outcomes, the exercise of free will becomes entwined in a cosmic orchestration where choices align with the existing state of affairs. The philosophical exploration extends to questions about the nature of choice within a framework that subtly directs the consequences of temporal actions.

Consider a time traveler faced with a decision that could potentially create a paradox. The act of choice, whether to alter the past or preserve its existing state, becomes a nuanced exploration of free will within the deterministic boundaries defined by the self-consistency principle. The philosophical inquiry navigates the labyrinth of temporal paradoxes, prompting reflection on the nature of agency when confronted with the imperative of self-consistent outcomes.

Ethical Dimensions: The Responsibility of Temporal Agency:

The philosophical exploration of free will and determinism within the context of time travel extends to ethical considerations. The ability to alter historical events introduces a dimension of responsibility that resonates with the exercise of agency. If individuals possess the power to reshape the past and influence the future, what ethical considerations should guide their choices?

Ethics within the temporal landscape prompts reflection on the consequences of temporal interventions. The exercise of free will, when entangled with the deterministic threads of causation, raises questions about the moral implications of altering the course of history. The philosophical exploration delves into the responsibility of temporal agency and the ethical boundaries that should govern the choices made within the corridors of time.

Consider a time traveler faced with the dilemma of whether to prevent a catastrophic event in the past. The act of choice becomes not only a reflection of free will but also a moral decision laden with consequences. The philosophical inquiry navigates the intersection of ethics, free will, and determinism within the temporal landscape, inviting contemplation on the ethical dimensions of wielding temporal power.

Temporal Morality: The Consequences of Altered Histories:

The altered histories resulting from temporal interventions raise philosophical questions about the nature of morality within the temporal landscape. If individuals possess the capacity to prevent or alter historical events, the consequences of their choices ripple through time, introducing ethical dimensions that resonate with the exercise of free will.

Philosophically, the consideration of temporal morality extends beyond the immediate consequences of altered histories. The act of altering the past, even with benevolent intentions, prompts reflection on the unintended consequences and unforeseen outcomes that may unfold across the corridors of time.

Consider a time traveler who, with the intention of preventing a tragedy, alters a key historical event. The act of choice, guided by free will, becomes a moral decision that shapes the narrative of temporal morality. The philosophical exploration navigates the consequences of altered histories, prompting contemplation on the ethical implications of reshaping the past.

Temporal Reflections: The Nature of Choice and Consciousness:

As we delve into the philosophical considerations of free will and determinism within the context of time travel, the nature of choice and consciousness becomes a focal point of inquiry. If individuals possess the capacity to make choices that reverberate through time, the philosophical exploration extends to questions about the enduring nature of consciousness within the temporal landscape.

Philosophically, the consideration of consciousness within the tapestry of time raises questions about the continuity of self-awareness across temporal dimensions. If choices made in the past shape the narrative of existence, does consciousness persist beyond the immediate present?

The exploration navigates the nuanced relationship between free will, determinism, and the enduring nature of consciousness within the corridors of time.

Conclusion: Philosophical Tapestry of Temporal Agency:

In the chapters that follow, we will continue our philosophical journey, dissecting additional considerations and delving into the broader implications of time travel on the human experience. Each layer peeled back reveals new facets of the philosophical tapestry of temporal agency, inviting us to explore the frontiers of free will and determinism within the realms of temporal manipulation.

Other philosophical paradoxes associated with time travel

As we venture deeper into the philosophical terrain of time travel, the tapestry of paradoxes unfolds, each strand revealing intricate questions that challenge our understanding of the universe. Beyond the Grandfather Paradox, other enigmatic riddles emerge, inviting us to navigate the twists and turns of conceptual landscapes where the past, present, and future entwine in paradoxical dance.

The Bootstrap Paradox: A Tapestry of Self-Creation:

At the heart of temporal conundrums lies the Bootstrap Paradox, an intricate tapestry that weaves questions about the origin of information and the recursive nature of causation. Imagine a scenario where an individual travels back in time and delivers information or an object to the past. If the delivered information becomes the basis for its own creation, a loop of self-creation ensues.

Philosophically, the Bootstrap Paradox prompts reflection on the origin of knowledge and artifacts within the temporal landscape. The very act of information or object delivery becomes a loop where the creation event lacks a clear origin. The philosophical exploration extends to questions about the nature of causation, self-creation, and the implications of a universe where certain events lack a discernible point of origin.

Consider a time traveler who imparts groundbreaking scientific knowledge to a historical figure, only to discover that the knowledge eventually leads to the creation of the time machine that facilitated the original journey. The act of imparting knowledge becomes a loop of self-creation, challenging our conventional notions of cause and effect within the temporal fabric.

The Ontological Paradox: The Interplay of Creation and Existence:

The Ontological Paradox delves into the intricate relationship between creation and existence within the context of time travel. This paradox unfolds when an individual travels back in time and interacts with a figure from the past, ultimately contributing to the creation of an object or entity that is crucial to the time traveler's own existence.

Philosophically, the Ontological Paradox raises questions about the interplay of agency and creation. The act of interacting with the past becomes a catalyst for the creation of essential elements that contribute to the time traveler's existence. The philosophical exploration extends to considerations of destiny, agency, and the delicate balance between creation and predestination.

Imagine a scenario where a time traveler collaborates with a historical artist to create a masterpiece that, in the future, becomes a pivotal artifact associated with the time traveler's identity. The interplay of creation and existence within the Ontological Paradox invites contemplation on the nature of agency and the intricate dance between contributing to and being shaped by one's own existence.

The Predestination Paradox: Destiny's Inescapable Embrace:

The Predestination Paradox immerses us in the notion that certain events in the past may be destined to occur, and attempts to alter them may inadvertently contribute to their fulfillment. This paradox suggests that the very act of time travel may be predetermined, entwining the traveler's actions with the events they seek to change.

Philosophically, the Predestination Paradox raises questions about the nature of free will and the possibility of escaping the inexorable pull of destiny. If attempts to alter the past merely contribute to the fulfillment of predetermined events, the philosophical exploration extends to considerations of agency, fate, and the complexities of navigating a temporal landscape where destiny's embrace may be inescapable.

Consider a time traveler who, driven by a desire to alter a critical historical event, inadvertently becomes a key participant in the unfolding of that very event. The attempt to change the course of history becomes a paradoxical journey where the traveler's actions contribute to the fulfillment of a destiny that appears to transcend individual agency.

The Information Paradox: Temporal Divergence and Inconsistencies:

The Information Paradox emerges from the complexities introduced by temporal divergence and the potential for inconsistencies within alternate timelines. This paradox explores scenarios where information from one timeline conflicts with or contradicts information from another, challenging our notions of a cohesive and consistent temporal reality.

Philosophically, the Information Paradox prompts reflection on the nature of truth and consistency within the temporal landscape. If divergent timelines lead to conflicting information, the philosophical exploration extends to considerations of reality, perception, and the challenges of reconciling disparate versions of historical events.

Consider a scenario where a time traveler, by altering a past event, creates a divergence that leads to the emergence of alternate timelines. The conflicting information across timelines becomes a philosophical puzzle, inviting contemplation on the nature of truth and the implications of a universe where different versions of history coexist.

The Eternal Return: Cyclical Narratives and Cosmic Repetition:

The concept of the Eternal Return introduces a philosophical paradigm where time is perceived as a cyclical narrative, endlessly repeating itself. This notion suggests that events, choices, and experiences may be destined to recur in an infinite loop, challenging our conventional understanding of linear time and the progression of history.

Philosophically, the Eternal Return prompts reflection on the nature of existence within a cyclic temporal framework. If time is eternally cyclical, the philosophical exploration extends to considerations of meaning, purpose, and the implications of a universe where every moment is destined to be endlessly replayed.

Consider a scenario where a time traveler, seeking to break free from the constraints of cyclical time, attempts to alter key events in the hope of disrupting the eternal recurrence. The philosophical inquiry navigates the complexities of cosmic repetition, inviting contemplation on the nature of individual agency within a universe where every action and consequence are fated to repeat in perpetuity.

The Butterfly Effect: Cascading Consequences and Unpredictable Outcomes:

While not exclusively a paradox associated with time travel, the Butterfly Effect becomes particularly pronounced within the temporal landscape. This concept, rooted in chaos theory, suggests that small changes in initial conditions can lead to vastly different outcomes. In the context of time travel, even seemingly insignificant alterations to the past may unleash cascading consequences with far-reaching and unpredictable outcomes.

Philosophically, the Butterfly Effect prompts reflection on the nature of causation, unpredictability, and the interconnectedness of events within the temporal landscape. The seemingly trivial choices made by a time traveler become catalysts for expansive and unpredictable consequences, challenging our ability to anticipate the intricate web of outcomes that may unfold.

Consider a time traveler who, with the intention of making a minor adjustment to a historical event, inadvertently sets off a chain reaction of consequences that reshape the course of history. The Butterfly Effect becomes a philosophical exploration of causation and the unpredictable nature of temporal interventions within the intricacies of the temporal fabric.

Conclusion: Navigating the Philosophical Labyrinth of Time:

As we navigate the twists and turns of paradoxes beyond time's veil, the philosophical landscape of time travel unfolds as a labyrinth of intricate inquiries. Each paradox invites us to unravel the mysteries of causation, agency, and the fundamental nature of reality within the temporal landscape. In the chapters that follow, we will delve into additional considerations, peeling back layers of conceptual complexity to explore the philosophical nuances that define the frontier between imagination and the enigmatic laws of time.

Examining how time travel challenges our understanding of the universe

As we venture into the realms of time travel, the philosophical underpinnings extend beyond specific paradoxes, inviting us to contemplate how this conceptual journey challenges the very foundations of our understanding of the universe. The exploration of time travel becomes a gateway to probing the fundamental nature of reality, causation, and the intricate tapestry that weaves together the cosmic narrative.

The Nature of Reality: Temporal Landscapes and Mutable Truths:

Time travel, with its potential to alter the past, introduces a profound challenge to our conventional notions of reality. The linear progression of events, etched into the historical record, is no longer a fixed and immutable narrative. The malleability of time suggests that reality itself may be subject to manipulation, raising questions about the nature of truth and the consistency of the universe.

Philosophically, the examination of how time travel challenges our understanding of reality prompts reflection on the dynamic relationship between perception and the temporal landscape. If the past is no longer a static canvas but a mutable tapestry, the philosophical exploration extends to considerations of the nature of truth and the implications of a universe where reality may be shaped by the choices made within the corridors of time.

Consider a scenario where a time traveler alters a critical historical event, creating a divergence in the timeline. The conflicting versions of reality across divergent timelines become a philosophical puzzle, inviting contemplation on the nature of truth and the challenges of reconciling disparate narratives within the temporal landscape.

Causation and the Cosmic Domino Effect:

Causation, the fundamental principle that links events in a chain of cause and effect, encounters a paradigm shift within the context of time travel. The linear progression of causation, once assumed to be an unbroken thread, becomes a complex tapestry where interventions in the past may unleash cascading consequences with far-reaching effects.

Philosophically, the examination of how time travel challenges our understanding of causation delves into the intricacies of the cosmic domino effect. If a seemingly minor alteration to the past can set off a chain reaction of consequences, the philosophical exploration extends to considerations of agency, unpredictability, and the interconnectedness of events within the temporal landscape.

Consider a time traveler who, with the intention of making a modest adjustment to a historical event, unknowingly initiates a sequence of events that reshape the course of history. The examination of causation becomes a philosophical inquiry into the nature of agency and the profound implications of interventions within the intricate web of cause and effect.

Temporal Relativity: Beyond the Arrow of Time:

The arrow of time, a concept rooted in the observed asymmetry of cause and effect, encounters challenges within the temporal landscape of time travel. The traditional linear progression from past to present to future becomes a canvas where individuals may traverse backward and forward, disrupting the chronological flow that defines our everyday experience.

Philosophically, the examination of how time travel challenges our understanding of the arrow of time prompts reflection on the relativity of temporal experiences. If individuals can navigate the past and the future, the philosophical exploration extends to considerations of the subjective nature of time and the implications of a universe where the arrow of time may be subject to manipulation.

Consider a scenario where a time traveler, by journeying to the past, witnesses events that occurred before their birth. The examination of temporal relativity becomes a philosophical inquiry into the nature of perception and the complex relationship between individual experiences and the chronological framework that governs our understanding of time.

Temporal Multiverse: Parallel Realities and Divergent Narratives:

The concept of a temporal multiverse emerges as a consequence of time travel, introducing the idea that divergent timelines and alternate realities coexist within the cosmic tapestry. The examination of how time travel challenges our understanding of the universe invites contemplation on the nature of existence across multiple timelines and the implications of a multiversal framework.

Philosophically, the exploration of the temporal multiverse extends to considerations of identity, agency, and the intricate dance between divergent narratives. If each temporal intervention leads to the creation of an alternative reality, the philosophical inquiry navigates the complexities of individual existence within a multiversal landscape.

Consider a time traveler who, through interventions in the past, creates divergent timelines where alternate versions of historical events unfold. The examination of the temporal multiverse becomes a philosophical inquiry into the nature of identity and the implications of a universe where individuals may exist across multiple realities.

Temporal Enigma: The Paradox of Immutability and Change:

The paradoxical nature of time travel challenges our conventional understanding of temporal immutability and the inevitability of change. The examination of how time travel challenges our understanding of the universe delves into the enigma of a reality where the past, once deemed unalterable, becomes a canvas for potential interventions.

Philosophically, the exploration of temporal enigma raises questions about the nature of inevitability and the implications of a universe where historical events may be subject to change. If individuals possess the power to alter the past, the philosophical inquiry extends to considerations of agency, responsibility, and the delicate balance between preservation and transformation within the temporal fabric.

Consider a scenario where a time traveler, faced with the opportunity to prevent a catastrophic event in the past, grapples with the ethical dimensions of altering the course of history. The examination of temporal enigma becomes a philosophical inquiry into the nature of responsibility and the complex interplay between the desire for change and the recognition of the inherent value of historical continuity.

Temporal Complexity: The Dance of Possibility and Impossibility:

The examination of how time travel challenges our understanding of the universe leads us into the realm of temporal complexity—a dance where the possible and the impossible intertwine within the cosmic narrative. The exploration of temporal complexity prompts reflection on the boundaries of what can be achieved within the temporal landscape and the intricate interplay between possibility and impossibility.

Philosophically, the examination of temporal complexity extends to considerations of human limitations and the implications of a universe where certain feats, once deemed impossible, may become achievable through temporal manipulation. The philosophical inquiry navigates the nuances of the dance between the conceivable and the inconceivable within the fabric of time.

Consider a time traveler who, by navigating the past, challenges the limits of what was once considered impossible. The examination of temporal complexity becomes a philosophical inquiry into the nature of human potential and the recognition that the boundaries of achievement within the temporal landscape may be subject to redefinition.

Conclusion: Beyond the Horizons of Temporal Inquiry:

As we conclude our exploration of how time travel challenges our understanding of the universe, the philosophical journey invites us to peer beyond the horizons of temporal inquiry. The intricate interplay between reality, causation, relativity, multiverses, enigmas, and complexity within the temporal landscape becomes a tapestry that unravels the fabric of our conventional understanding. In the chapters that follow, we will continue our philosophical odyssey, delving into additional considerations that shape the frontiers of temporal exploration and redefine our perception of the universe.

Chapter 3: Scientific Challenges
Technological barriers to achieving time travel

The quest for time travel, while captivating the imagination, is beset by a myriad of technological hurdles that appear insurmountable within the current scope of scientific understanding. This chapter delves into the intricate tapestry of technological barriers, exploring the daunting challenges that stand as formidable gatekeepers on the path to temporal manipulation.

Temporal Mechanics: The Fundamental Enigma of Time Control:

At the heart of technological barriers to achieving time travel lies the elusive mastery of temporal mechanics—the ability to manipulate time at will. The examination of temporal mechanics involves grappling with the very fabric of spacetime, understanding its curvature, and developing methodologies to bend it according to human intentions.

Philosophically, the pursuit of temporal mechanics raises questions about the limits of human knowledge and the audacity of attempting to control a fundamental aspect of the universe. If time is indeed a dimension that can be molded and shaped, the technological exploration extends to considerations of the ethical dimensions of wielding such power over the very essence of existence.

Consider a scenario where scientists, armed with a theoretical understanding of temporal mechanics, embark on experiments to manipulate localized spacetime. The philosophical inquiry into the technological challenges of time travel becomes a reflection on the audacious endeavor to control a dimension that has shaped the cosmic narrative since the inception of the universe.

Energy Requirements: Harnessing the Power of Temporal Manipulation:

The staggering energy requirements for achieving time travel pose a monumental challenge that stretches the limits of current technological capabilities. The examination of energy requirements involves not only identifying the immense power needed to manipulate spacetime but also devising methods to harness and direct this energy with precision.

Philosophically, the exploration of energy requirements for time travel delves into the ethical considerations of harnessing vast amounts of energy for a singular purpose. If the manipulation of time demands unprecedented energy sources, the technological inquiry extends to reflections on the responsible and sustainable use of such power.

Consider a scenario where scientists, in pursuit of time travel, engineer colossal energy-generation systems to meet the demands of temporal manipulation. The philosophical inquiry into energy requirements becomes a contemplation on the responsibility of wielding immense power in the pursuit of unlocking the secrets of time.

Temporal Navigation: Navigating the Labyrinth of Temporal Coordinates:

Navigating through time requires the development of precise temporal coordinates—an intricate system that allows individuals or objects to traverse specific points in the temporal landscape. The examination of temporal navigation involves understanding the complexities of spacetime coordinates and devising methods for accurate and controlled temporal displacement.

Philosophically, the exploration of temporal navigation raises questions about the nature of destination and the implications of venturing into the unknown realms of the past and the future. If temporal coordinates become the map for time travelers, the technological inquiry extends to considerations of the ethical dimensions of exploring uncharted territories within the temporal landscape.

Consider a scenario where scientists, equipped with advanced temporal navigation systems, send probes into the past and the future. The philosophical inquiry into temporal navigation becomes a reflection on the responsibility of navigating the labyrinth of time and the potential consequences of venturing into temporal territories that may hold unforeseen challenges.

Temporal Stability: Avoiding Cataclysmic Temporal Anomalies:

The pursuit of time travel technology introduces the perilous challenge of ensuring temporal stability—a safeguard against catastrophic temporal anomalies that could disrupt the fabric of spacetime. The examination of temporal stability involves developing methods to prevent unintended consequences, paradoxes, and disruptions caused by temporal interventions.

Philosophically, the exploration of temporal stability raises questions about the consequences of manipulating time and the responsibility of safeguarding the integrity of the temporal landscape. If unintended anomalies can lead to chaos, the technological inquiry extends to reflections on the ethical considerations of mitigating the risks associated with temporal manipulation.

Consider a scenario where scientists, in their pursuit of time travel, implement robust temporal stability protocols to prevent unintended consequences. The philosophical inquiry into temporal stability becomes a contemplation on the responsibility of temporal engineers to ensure the preservation of the cosmic narrative while venturing into uncharted territories within the temporal landscape.

Temporal Synchronization: Aligning Time Travel with Cosmic Rhythms:

Achieving temporal synchronization—the ability to align temporal manipulations with the cosmic rhythms of the universe—poses a significant technological challenge. The examination of temporal synchronization involves understanding the intricate interplay between local temporal interventions and the broader cosmic timeline.

Philosophically, the exploration of temporal synchronization raises questions about the relationship between individual temporal actions and the cosmic narrative. If time travel is to coexist harmoniously with the natural flow of the universe, the technological inquiry extends to considerations of the ethical dimensions of temporal engineering within the broader context of cosmic rhythms.

Consider a scenario where scientists, in their pursuit of time travel, develop technologies that synchronize temporal interventions with the natural rhythms of the universe. The philosophical inquiry into temporal synchronization becomes a reflection on the responsibility of temporal engineers to align their actions with the cosmic dance of spacetime.

Temporal Observability: The Challenge of Witnessing Temporal Manipulations:

Observing the outcomes of temporal manipulations presents a unique technological challenge, as the very act of witnessing such interventions may introduce complexities. The examination of temporal observability involves developing methods to capture, analyze, and comprehend the effects of temporal actions without disrupting the natural flow of the temporal landscape.

Philosophically, the exploration of temporal observability raises questions about the nature of knowledge and the implications of observing the consequences of time travel. If the act of observation influences the outcomes of temporal interventions, the technological inquiry extends to considerations of the ethical dimensions of knowledge acquisition within the temporal landscape.

Consider a scenario where scientists, in their pursuit of time travel, devise advanced observational techniques to study the effects of temporal manipulations. The philosophical inquiry into temporal observability becomes a contemplation on the responsibility of temporal engineers to acquire knowledge without unduly influencing the outcomes of their interventions.

Temporal Ethics: Navigating the Moral Dimensions of Time Travel Technology:

The overarching technological challenge in the pursuit of time travel lies in navigating the intricate moral dimensions inherent in wielding the power to manipulate time. The examination of temporal ethics involves developing frameworks and guidelines that guide the responsible and ethical use of time travel technology.

Philosophically, the exploration of temporal ethics raises fundamental questions about the consequences of time manipulation on the human experience and the ethical responsibilities of those who possess the knowledge and technology to alter the course of history. The technological inquiry extends to considerations of the ethical dimensions of wielding power over the very fabric of existence.

Consider a scenario where scientists, in their pursuit of time travel, establish ethical guidelines that govern the responsible use of temporal manipulation. The philosophical inquiry into temporal ethics becomes a reflection on the responsibility of temporal engineers to balance the pursuit of knowledge with the preservation of the moral fabric that defines human existence.

Conclusion: The Uncharted Frontiers of Temporal Engineering:

As we conclude our exploration of the technological barriers to achieving time travel, the technological challenges emerge as formidable gatekeepers guarding the uncharted frontiers of temporal manipulation. The intricate interplay between temporal mechanics, energy requirements, navigation, stability, synchronization, observability, and ethics defines the landscape where temporal engineers strive to unlock the secrets of time. In the chapters that follow, we will continue our technological odyssey, delving into additional considerations that shape the frontiers of temporal engineering and redefine our perception of what may be achievable within the temporal landscape.

Energy requirements and the impracticality of generating the necessary power

The endeavor to unravel the mysteries of time travel confronts an imposing adversary—the staggering energy requirements necessary for manipulating the fabric of spacetime. As we delve into the heart of scientific challenges, the impracticality of generating the colossal power demanded by time travel technology becomes a central focus, revealing a profound barrier that tests the limits of our scientific imagination.

Temporal Manipulation and the Essence of Energy:

At the core of the impracticality of time travel lies the essence of energy— a fundamental force that dictates the dynamics of the universe. Temporal manipulation, requiring the bending and shaping of spacetime, demands energy on a scale that dwarfs conventional notions of power generation. The examination of energy requirements delves into the intricacies of harnessing and directing vast amounts of energy to sculpt the temporal landscape.

Philosophically, the exploration of energy requirements for time travel prompts reflection on the audacity of attempting to control a force as fundamental as energy. If time travel hinges on the ability to commandeer unparalleled amounts of power, the scientific inquiry extends to considerations of the ethical dimensions of wielding such extraordinary energy for a singular purpose.

Consider a scenario where scientists, in their pursuit of temporal manipulation, grapple with the fundamental question of how to harness the essence of energy to bend the fabric of spacetime. The philosophical inquiry into energy requirements becomes a reflection on the audacious endeavor to commandeer the very force that propels the cosmic narrative.

Temporal Energy Quotient: Unraveling the Cosmic Equation:

The impracticality of generating the necessary power for time travel introduces the concept of the temporal energy quotient—an intricate equation that balances the demands of temporal manipulation with the available reservoirs of energy. The examination of the energy quotient involves deciphering the cosmic equation that governs the feasibility of time travel and exploring the delicate balance between ambition and scientific reality.

Philosophically, the exploration of the temporal energy quotient raises questions about the hubris of attempting to solve a cosmic equation that may be beyond the grasp of human understanding. If the temporal energy quotient becomes the arbiter of time travel feasibility, the scientific inquiry extends to considerations of humility in the face of cosmic complexity.

Consider a scenario where scientists, in their pursuit of time travel, strive to unravel the temporal energy quotient—a cosmic equation that defines the limits of temporal manipulation. The philosophical inquiry into the energy quotient becomes a reflection on the humility required to navigate the uncharted territories of spacetime and the recognition that some cosmic equations may remain inscrutable.

Energy Reservoirs: Tapping into Cosmic Wellsprings:

The impracticality of generating the necessary power for time travel propels scientists into the realm of energy reservoirs—cosmic wellsprings that hold the potential to fuel the monumental requirements of temporal manipulation. The examination of energy reservoirs involves identifying, tapping into, and harnessing the colossal sources of energy dispersed throughout the universe.

Philosophically, the exploration of energy reservoirs raises questions about the responsibility of tapping into cosmic wellsprings and the potential consequences of redirecting vast amounts of energy for the singular purpose of time travel. If energy reservoirs become the lifeline for temporal manipulation, the scientific inquiry extends to considerations of the ethical dimensions of accessing cosmic wellsprings for human ambitions.

Consider a scenario where scientists, in their pursuit of time travel, discover and harness energy reservoirs scattered across the cosmos. The philosophical inquiry into energy reservoirs becomes a reflection on the responsibility of temporal engineers to navigate the ethical complexities of redirecting cosmic energy for the advancement of human knowledge.

Quantum Energetics: Navigating the Subatomic Seas of Power:

Quantum energetics emerges as a frontier within the landscape of time travel, offering glimpses into the subatomic seas of power that may hold the key to surmounting energy requirements. The examination of quantum energetics involves probing the fundamental nature of energy at the quantum level and exploring methods to manipulate quantum states for the generation of colossal power.

Philosophically, the exploration of quantum energetics raises questions about the ethical considerations of delving into the subatomic realm and the potential consequences of wielding quantum forces for temporal manipulation. If quantum energetics becomes the pathway to unlocking the necessary power for time travel, the scientific inquiry extends to reflections on the responsibility of navigating the uncharted territories of quantum power.

Consider a scenario where scientists, in their pursuit of time travel, navigate the subatomic seas of quantum energetics to unlock new sources of power. The philosophical inquiry into quantum energetics becomes a reflection on the ethical considerations of venturing into the quantum realm and the recognition that quantum forces may hold both promise and peril.

Temporal Sustainability: Balancing Ambition with Cosmic Harmony:

The impracticality of generating the necessary power for time travel introduces the imperative of temporal sustainability—a commitment to balance the ambitions of temporal manipulation with the harmony of the cosmic narrative. The examination of temporal sustainability involves developing methodologies that ensure the responsible and sustainable use of energy for time travel, considering the long-term consequences of temporal interventions on the cosmic order.

Philosophically, the exploration of temporal sustainability raises questions about the responsibility of temporal engineers to consider the ecological impact of their endeavors and the potential consequences of disrupting the delicate balance of the cosmic narrative. If temporal sustainability becomes a guiding principle, the scientific inquiry extends to reflections on the ethical dimensions of temporal engineering within the broader context of cosmic harmony.

Consider a scenario where scientists, in their pursuit of time travel, establish principles of temporal sustainability to guide their endeavors. The philosophical inquiry into temporal sustainability becomes a reflection on the responsibility of temporal engineers to navigate the ethical complexities of temporal manipulation while preserving the ecological balance of the cosmic narrative.

Temporal Ethics of Power: Navigating the Moral Dimensions of Temporal Energy:

The overarching challenge in the impracticality of generating the necessary power for time travel lies in navigating the intricate moral dimensions inherent in wielding the colossal power required for temporal manipulation. The examination of temporal ethics of power involves developing frameworks and guidelines that guide the responsible and ethical use of energy for time travel, considering the moral implications of harnessing vast amounts of power for the advancement of human knowledge.

Philosophically, the exploration of temporal ethics of power raises fundamental questions about the consequences of wielding extraordinary energy for temporal manipulation and the ethical responsibilities of those who possess the knowledge and technology to alter the course of history. If temporal ethics of power become the guiding principles, the scientific inquiry extends to considerations of the ethical dimensions of wielding colossal power over the very fabric of existence.

Consider a scenario where scientists, in their pursuit of time travel, establish ethical guidelines that govern the responsible use of energy for temporal manipulation. The philosophical inquiry into temporal ethics of power becomes a reflection on the responsibility of temporal engineers to balance the pursuit of knowledge with the preservation of the moral fabric that defines human existence.

Conclusion: The Boundless Horizons of Temporal Power:

As we conclude our exploration of the impracticality of generating the necessary power for time travel, the scientific challenges emerge as formidable gatekeepers guarding the boundless horizons of temporal power. The intricate interplay between temporal manipulation, energy requirements, energy reservoirs, quantum energetics, temporal sustainability, and temporal ethics of power defines the landscape where temporal engineers strive to unlock the secrets of time. In the chapters that follow, we will continue our scientific odyssey, delving into additional considerations that shape the frontiers of temporal power and redefine our perception of what may be achievable within the temporal landscape.

Time dilation and the difficulties associated with achieving the required speeds

The journey into the scientific challenges of time travel unravels yet another enigma—the intricate relationship between time dilation and the formidable difficulties associated with achieving the required speeds. As we navigate the relativistic seas, the concept of time dilation becomes a central focus, exposing the complexities that arise when attempting to breach the cosmic barriers that separate us from the past and the future.

Time Dilation Unveiled: The Relativistic Warp of Temporal Fabric:

At the heart of the difficulties associated with achieving the required speeds for time travel lies the phenomenon of time dilation—a relativistic effect predicted by Einstein's theory of general relativity. Time dilation posits that as an object approaches the speed of light, time for that object appears to pass more slowly relative to a stationary observer. The examination of time dilation unveils the relativistic warp in the fabric of spacetime, introducing a fundamental challenge to the aspirations of temporal exploration.

Philosophically, the exploration of time dilation raises questions about the nature of time itself and the implications of relative experiences within the temporal landscape. If time dilation becomes a tangible effect, the scientific inquiry extends to considerations of the philosophical dimensions of time and the intricate interplay between perception and reality within the relativistic framework.

Consider a scenario where scientists, in their pursuit of time travel, grapple with the implications of time dilation—a phenomenon that challenges the conventional understanding of time as a universal constant. The philosophical inquiry into time dilation becomes a reflection on the audacity of manipulating time within the relativistic seas and the recognition that temporal experiences may be inherently subjective.

Relativistic Speeds: Approaching the Cosmic Speed Limit:

Achieving the required speeds for time travel involves pushing the boundaries of what is conventionally considered feasible in the realm of physics. The examination of relativistic speeds delves into the concept of approaching the cosmic speed limit— the speed of light. As an object accelerates toward the speed of light, the relativistic effects become increasingly pronounced, introducing complexities that hinder the seamless navigation of spacetime.

Philosophically, the exploration of relativistic speeds raises questions about the nature of cosmic boundaries and the challenges of breaching the conventional limits imposed by the cosmic speed limit. If achieving relativistic speeds becomes a prerequisite for temporal manipulation, the scientific inquiry extends to considerations of the philosophical dimensions of cosmic boundaries and the audacity of attempting to transcend them.

Consider a scenario where scientists, in their pursuit of time travel, embark on experiments to approach relativistic speeds—accelerating objects to a significant fraction of the speed of light. The philosophical inquiry into relativistic speeds becomes a reflection on the audacity of challenging the cosmic speed limit and the recognition that the journey toward temporal exploration may demand a willingness to confront the fundamental limits of the universe.

Einstein's Relativity: Temporal Dimensions in Motion:

Einstein's theory of relativity serves as the guiding framework for understanding the relativistic effects associated with achieving the required speeds for time travel. The examination of Einstein's relativity involves delving into the equations that describe the relationship between time, space, and motion at relativistic speeds. The theory provides the foundation for comprehending the temporal distortions that arise as objects approach the speed of light.

Philosophically, the exploration of Einstein's relativity raises questions about the nature of spacetime and the conceptual shift introduced by a theory that unifies space and time into a single, dynamic fabric. If Einstein's relativity becomes the cornerstone for temporal exploration, the scientific inquiry extends to considerations of the philosophical dimensions of a universe where the very nature of reality is intricately linked to motion and relative perspectives.

Consider a scenario where scientists, in their pursuit of time travel, immerse themselves in the equations of Einstein's relativity, seeking to unlock the secrets of spacetime manipulation. The philosophical inquiry into Einstein's relativity becomes a reflection on the transformative power of a theory that redefines our understanding of the fabric of the universe and the potential implications for navigating the temporal landscape.

Cosmic Speed Limitations: The Imposing Barrier of Light's Dominion:

The difficulties associated with achieving the required speeds for time travel become pronounced when confronted with the imposing barrier of light's dominion—the cosmic speed limit. The examination of cosmic speed limitations involves grappling with the fundamental constraint imposed by the speed of light, which serves as a universal constant and an unyielding boundary within the fabric of spacetime.

Philosophically, the exploration of cosmic speed limitations raises questions about the nature of universal constants and the challenges of confronting an absolute barrier within the temporal landscape. If the speed of light becomes an insurmountable threshold for temporal exploration, the scientific inquiry extends to considerations of the philosophical dimensions of universal constraints and the audacity of challenging the cosmic speed limit.

Consider a scenario where scientists, in their pursuit of time travel, confront the cosmic speed limit—the ultimate barrier that dictates the maximum speed attainable in the universe. The philosophical inquiry into cosmic speed limitations becomes a reflection on the audacity of challenging the very limits of cosmic speed and the recognition that the journey toward temporal exploration may demand a willingness to confront absolute boundaries.

Warping Spacetime: Navigating Relativistic Trajectories:

Navigating the relativistic trajectories required for time travel involves the concept of warping spacetime—a theoretical framework that envisions manipulating the curvature of spacetime to create pathways for temporal displacement. The examination of warping spacetime delves into the intricacies of bending the fabric of the universe to create shortcuts and corridors that allow for faster-than-light travel.

Philosophically, the exploration of warping spacetime raises questions about the nature of spacetime manipulation and the potential consequences of bending the fabric of the universe. If warping spacetime becomes the method for achieving relativistic trajectories, the scientific inquiry extends to considerations of the philosophical dimensions of manipulating the very structure of reality and the audacity of attempting to reshape the cosmic narrative.

Consider a scenario where scientists, in their pursuit of time travel, explore the theoretical possibilities of warping spacetime—a method that challenges the conventional understanding of the static nature of the universe. The philosophical inquiry into warping spacetime becomes a reflection on the audacity of manipulating the fabric of reality itself and the recognition that the journey toward temporal exploration may demand a willingness to navigate uncharted territories within the conceptual landscape of spacetime.

Temporal Navigation: The Challenges of Precision and Control:

Achieving the required speeds for time travel introduces the challenges of precision and control in navigating the relativistic trajectories. The examination of temporal navigation involves developing methodologies to ensure accurate and controlled displacement within the temporal landscape, considering the complexities introduced by relativistic effects and the need for precision in temporal interventions.

Philosophically, the exploration of temporal navigation raises questions about the nature of control within the relativistic seas of spacetime and the potential consequences of imprecise temporal displacements. If temporal navigation becomes a crucial aspect of achieving relativistic trajectories, the scientific inquiry extends to considerations of the philosophical dimensions of control and precision within the dynamic framework of the temporal landscape.

Consider a scenario where scientists, in their pursuit of time travel, focus on the challenges of temporal navigation—developing technologies that allow for accurate and controlled displacement within the relativistic seas. The philosophical inquiry into temporal navigation becomes a reflection on the responsibility of temporal engineers to navigate the complexities of spacetime with precision and the recognition that the journey toward temporal exploration may demand a willingness to confront the challenges of control within the dynamic fabric of the universe.

Temporal Ethics of Relativity: Navigating the Moral Dimensions of Relativistic Trajectories:

The overarching challenge in the difficulties associated with achieving the required speeds for time travel lies in navigating the intricate moral dimensions inherent in breaching the cosmic speed limit and manipulating the fabric of spacetime. The examination of temporal ethics of relativity involves developing frameworks and guidelines that guide the responsible and ethical use of relativistic trajectories for time travel, considering the moral implications of challenging fundamental cosmic boundaries.

Philosophically, the exploration of temporal ethics of relativity raises fundamental questions about the consequences of manipulating the fabric of the universe and the ethical responsibilities of those who possess the knowledge and technology to alter the course of history. If temporal ethics of relativity become the guiding principles, the scientific inquiry extends to considerations of the ethical dimensions of wielding power over the very fabric of existence.

Consider a scenario where scientists, in their pursuit of time travel, establish ethical guidelines that govern the responsible use of relativistic trajectories for temporal manipulation. The philosophical inquiry into temporal ethics of relativity becomes a reflection on the responsibility of temporal engineers to balance the pursuit of knowledge with the preservation of the moral fabric that defines human existence.

Conclusion: The Relativistic Odyssey of Temporal Exploration:

As we conclude our exploration of time dilation and the difficulties associated with achieving the required speeds for time travel, the scientific challenges emerge as formidable gatekeepers guarding the relativistic odyssey of temporal exploration. The intricate interplay between time dilation, relativistic speeds, Einstein's relativity, cosmic speed limitations, warping spacetime, temporal navigation, and temporal ethics of relativity defines the landscape where temporal engineers strive to unlock the secrets of time. In the chapters that follow, we will continue our scientific odyssey, delving into additional considerations that shape the frontiers of temporal exploration and redefine our perception of what may be achievable within the relativistic seas of the temporal landscape.

Scientific arguments against the feasibility of time travel

Amidst the tantalizing prospects and philosophical musings surrounding time travel, a chorus of skepticism emerges from the scientific community. This chapter delves into the scientific arguments against the feasibility of time travel, scrutinizing the theoretical, physical, and practical challenges that cast doubt upon the realization of temporal exploration.

The Arrow of Time: Unyielding Dictator of Temporal Flow:

One of the foundational scientific arguments against time travel rests upon the concept of the arrow of time—a relentless force that dictates the irreversible flow of temporal events. According to this argument, time travel would require a reversal or manipulation of the arrow of time, a feat deemed incompatible with our current understanding of the laws of physics.

Philosophically, the exploration of the arrow of time raises questions about the nature of causality and the implications of attempting to defy a fundamental force that governs the cosmic narrative. If the arrow of time proves insurmountable, the scientific inquiry extends to considerations of the philosophical dimensions of time as an immutable and linear force.

Consider a scenario where scientists, in their pursuit of time travel, grapple with the challenge posed by the arrow of time—a force that resists any attempt to reverse or manipulate the natural flow of events. The philosophical inquiry into the arrow of time becomes a reflection on the audacity of challenging the very essence of temporal causality and the recognition that time, as we perceive it, may be an unyielding dictator of the cosmic narrative.

Quantum Mechanics and Entanglement: The Enigma of Temporal Superposition:

The realm of quantum mechanics introduces another scientific argument against the feasibility of time travel, stemming from the principles of superposition and entanglement. Quantum mechanics suggests that particles can exist in multiple states simultaneously, a phenomenon known as superposition. Critics argue that applying these principles to macroscopic objects, particularly within the context of time travel, poses significant conceptual and practical challenges.

Philosophically, the exploration of quantum mechanics and entanglement raises questions about the nature of reality and the potential consequences of attempting to extend quantum principles to the macroscopic world of temporal exploration. If superposition and entanglement prove elusive in the context of time travel, the scientific inquiry extends to considerations of the philosophical dimensions of quantum mechanics within the cosmic framework.

Consider a scenario where scientists, in their pursuit of time travel, confront the enigma of temporal superposition—a challenge that tests the applicability of quantum principles to the vast scales involved in manipulating time. The philosophical inquiry into quantum mechanics and entanglement becomes a reflection on the audacity of extending quantum concepts to the cosmic narrative and the recognition that the microscopic intricacies of quantum reality may resist seamless integration into the macroscopic fabric of time.

Grandfather Paradox: Temporal Self-Consistency Under Scrutiny:

A perennial conundrum in the discourse on time travel is the Grandfather Paradox—an apparent logical contradiction that arises when a hypothetical time traveler interacts with past events in a way that prevents their own existence. Scientifically, the Grandfather Paradox raises questions about the self-consistency of temporal events and challenges the coherence of a universe where such paradoxes could occur.

Philosophically, the exploration of the Grandfather Paradox raises questions about the nature of causality and the potential consequences of altering past events within the context of time travel. If the Grandfather Paradox remains unresolved, the scientific inquiry extends to considerations of the philosophical dimensions of causality and the intricate web of temporal events that define the cosmic narrative.

Consider a scenario where scientists, in their pursuit of time travel, grapple with the implications of the Grandfather Paradox—a scenario that challenges the very fabric of self-consistent temporal narratives. The philosophical inquiry into the Grandfather Paradox becomes a reflection on the audacity of navigating the intricacies of causality within the temporal landscape and the recognition that the coherence of time may demand a more nuanced understanding of the relationship between past, present, and future.

Temporal Uncertainty and Observer Effects: The Elusive Nature of Time Measurement:

The principles of temporal uncertainty, drawn from the Heisenberg Uncertainty Principle in quantum mechanics, introduce skepticism regarding the precision and reliability of measuring time intervals in the context of time travel. Critics argue that the very act of observing and measuring temporal events may introduce uncertainties that render precise manipulation of time an elusive endeavor.

Philosophically, the exploration of temporal uncertainty and observer effects raises questions about the nature of knowledge and the potential consequences of attempting to measure time with absolute precision. If temporal uncertainty remains an inherent aspect of time measurement, the scientific inquiry extends to considerations of the philosophical dimensions of knowledge acquisition within the temporal landscape.

Consider a scenario where scientists, in their pursuit of time travel, confront the challenges posed by temporal uncertainty and observer effects—a scenario that questions the very foundations of our ability to measure and manipulate time. The philosophical inquiry into temporal uncertainty becomes a reflection on the audacity of acquiring knowledge within the dynamic framework of the temporal landscape and the recognition that the very act of observation may introduce complexities that challenge the precision of temporal measurements.

Energy Requirements and Technological Constraints: The Insurmountable Barrier of Power:

Practical limitations, particularly those related to energy requirements, form a robust scientific argument against the feasibility of time travel. Critics contend that the colossal amounts of energy needed to manipulate spacetime, as envisioned in various time travel theories, surpass our current technological capabilities and may remain insurmountable within the foreseeable future.

Philosophically, the exploration of energy requirements and technological constraints raises questions about the limits of human ingenuity and the potential consequences of attempting to overcome practical barriers within the context of time travel. If energy requirements prove prohibitive, the scientific inquiry extends to considerations of the philosophical dimensions of technological progress and the audacity of challenging the limits of our current understanding.

Consider a scenario where scientists, in their pursuit of time travel, grapple with the challenges posed by energy requirements and technological constraints—a scenario that tests the boundaries of human innovation. The philosophical inquiry into energy requirements becomes a reflection on the audacity of challenging the limits of technological progress within the dynamic landscape of the temporal exploration and the recognition that practical barriers may impose constraints on our aspirations.

Challenges of Temporal Engineering: Navigating the Complexity of Time Manipulation:

The overarching scientific argument against the feasibility of time travel revolves around the complexities of temporal engineering itself. Critics assert that the very nature of manipulating time introduces inherent challenges, both theoretically and practically, that may render precise and controlled temporal interventions an unattainable goal.

Philosophically, the exploration of the challenges of temporal engineering raises questions about the nature of control within the temporal landscape and the potential consequences of attempting to reshape the fabric of reality. If the challenges of temporal engineering prove formidable, the scientific inquiry extends to considerations of the philosophical dimensions of human agency within the dynamic framework of temporal exploration.

Consider a scenario where scientists, in their pursuit of time travel, confront the intricacies of temporal engineering—a scenario that demands a nuanced understanding of the complexities inherent in manipulating time. The philosophical inquiry into the challenges of temporal engineering becomes a reflection on the audacity of reshaping the very nature of reality and the recognition that the journey toward temporal exploration may demand a willingness to navigate the uncharted territories of temporal engineering.

Conclusion: The Skeptical Echoes of Temporal Doubt:

As we conclude our exploration of scientific arguments against the feasibility of time travel, the skeptical echoes of temporal doubt reverberate within the scientific discourse. The intricate interplay between the arrow of time, quantum mechanics and entanglement, the Grandfather Paradox, temporal uncertainty and observer effects, energy requirements and technological constraints, and the challenges of temporal engineering defines the landscape where temporal engineers grapple with the complexities of reshaping the fabric of reality. In the chapters that follow, we will continue our journey, exploring additional considerations that shape the frontiers of temporal exploration and redefine our perception of what may be achievable within the dynamic framework of the temporal landscape.

Chapter 4: Historical Impact
Chaos and disruptions in historical events if time travel were possible

The prospect of time travel tantalizes the human imagination with visions of revisiting the past or glimpsing into the future. However, beneath the allure lies a sobering consideration—what if time travel were possible, and what chaos and disruptions might unfold in historical events as a consequence?

Temporal Intervention: A Butterfly's Flutter and the Hurricane of Change:

One of the pivotal concerns surrounding time travel is the potential for small, seemingly inconsequential actions to trigger monumental changes—a phenomenon often referred to as the "butterfly effect." The exploration of chaos and disruptions in historical events begins with an examination of the butterfly effect, where even the subtlest of interventions may send ripples through time, reshaping the course of events in unforeseen ways.

Philosophically, the consideration of the butterfly effect raises questions about the nature of causality and the potential consequences of seemingly minor actions within the context of historical events. If the butterfly effect proves pervasive, the exploration extends to considerations of the philosophical dimensions of agency and the intricate web of causation that defines the cosmic narrative.

Consider a scenario where time travelers, in their attempts to observe or influence historical events, inadvertently set in motion a cascade of changes—a scenario that challenges the deterministic view of history and introduces the unpredictable dynamics of temporal intervention. The philosophical inquiry into the butterfly effect becomes a reflection on the audacity of navigating the intricacies of causality within the temporal landscape and the recognition that seemingly insignificant actions may carry profound consequences.

Historical Integrity: The Fragility of Recorded Narratives:

Time travel introduces the prospect of tampering with historical records and narratives—an act that threatens the very integrity of our understanding of the past. The examination of chaos and disruptions in historical events involves considering the fragility of recorded histories and the potential consequences of altering or erasing key moments that have shaped civilizations.

Philosophically, the exploration of historical integrity raises questions about the nature of knowledge and the potential consequences of tampering with the historical record within the context of time travel. If historical integrity proves vulnerable, the exploration extends to considerations of the philosophical dimensions of truth and the challenges of preserving the authenticity of historical narratives.

Consider a scenario where time travelers, in their attempts to observe or influence historical events, inadvertently alter key moments in recorded history—a scenario that tests the resilience of our understanding of the past. The philosophical inquiry into historical integrity becomes a reflection on the audacity of navigating the complexities of historical knowledge within the temporal landscape and the recognition that the preservation of truth may demand a nuanced understanding of the relationship between past, present, and future.

Temporal Paradoxes: The Tapestry of Causality Unraveling:

The potential for time travel to create paradoxes—logical contradictions that defy the conventional understanding of causality—forms a central theme in considering chaos and disruptions in historical events. The exploration of temporal paradoxes involves unraveling the tapestry of causality itself, where actions in the past may lead to contradictory outcomes or render historical narratives incoherent.

Philosophically, the consideration of temporal paradoxes raises questions about the nature of reality and the potential consequences of navigating a landscape where logical contradictions may emerge within the context of time travel. If temporal paradoxes prove unavoidable, the exploration extends to considerations of the philosophical dimensions of causality and the intricate web of temporal events that define the cosmic narrative.

Consider a scenario where time travelers, in their attempts to observe or influence historical events, inadvertently create paradoxes—a scenario that challenges the conventional understanding of causality and introduces the perplexing dynamics of temporal contradictions. The philosophical inquiry into temporal paradoxes becomes a reflection on the audacity of navigating the intricacies of logical coherence within the temporal landscape and the recognition that the preservation of a coherent narrative may demand a more nuanced understanding of the relationship between past, present, and future.

Unintended Consequences: The Ripple Effect of Historical Interference:

The notion of unintended consequences looms large when contemplating the chaos and disruptions that might arise from historical interference through time travel. The examination of unintended consequences involves considering how seemingly well-intentioned actions in the past may lead to unforeseen and undesirable outcomes, creating a ripple effect that extends far beyond the initial intervention.

Philosophically, the exploration of unintended consequences raises questions about the nature of human agency and the potential consequences of attempting to shape historical events within the context of time travel. If unintended consequences prove inevitable, the exploration extends to considerations of the philosophical dimensions of agency and the intricate interplay between human intentions and the dynamic framework of the temporal landscape.

Consider a scenario where time travelers, in their attempts to observe or influence historical events, inadvertently set in motion unintended consequences—a scenario that challenges the notion of control within the temporal landscape and introduces the complexities of unforeseen outcomes. The philosophical inquiry into unintended consequences becomes a reflection on the audacity of navigating the intricacies of human agency within the temporal landscape and the recognition that the pursuit of well-intentioned actions may demand a humility in the face of temporal uncertainties.

Cultural Shifts and Paradigm Changes: The Ripple Effect on Societies:

Temporal interventions can extend beyond individual actions to reshape entire societies, triggering cultural shifts and paradigm changes. The exploration of chaos and disruptions in historical events involves considering how alterations in key moments may lead to divergent timelines, where societies evolve along different trajectories, fostering distinct values, beliefs, and norms.

Philosophically, the consideration of cultural shifts and paradigm changes raises questions about the nature of societal evolution and the potential consequences of reshaping historical events within the context of time travel. If cultural shifts prove pervasive, the exploration extends to considerations of the philosophical dimensions of cultural identity and the challenges of navigating the dynamic framework of societal development.

Consider a scenario where time travelers, in their attempts to observe or influence historical events, inadvertently foster cultural shifts and paradigm changes—a scenario that challenges the notion of societal determinism and introduces the complexities of divergent timelines. The philosophical inquiry into cultural shifts becomes a reflection on the audacity of navigating the intricacies of societal evolution within the temporal landscape and the recognition that the pursuit of societal well-being may demand an awareness of the potential ripple effects of temporal interventions.

Ethical Dilemmas: The Morality of Historical Intervention:

The chaos and disruptions in historical events through time travel raise profound ethical dilemmas, as the actions of time travelers may impact the lives of individuals and alter the course of entire civilizations. The examination of ethical dilemmas involves considering the moral implications of historical interventions and the responsibilities that come with the power to shape the past.

Philosophically, the exploration of ethical dilemmas raises questions about the nature of moral agency and the potential consequences of attempting to influence historical events within the context of time travel. If ethical dilemmas prove inherent to temporal intervention, the exploration extends to considerations of the philosophical dimensions of moral responsibility and the challenges of navigating the dynamic framework of ethical decision-making.

Consider a scenario where time travelers, in their attempts to observe or influence historical events, confront profound ethical dilemmas—a scenario that tests the boundaries of moral agency within the temporal landscape. The philosophical inquiry into ethical dilemmas becomes a reflection on the audacity of navigating the intricacies of moral responsibility within the temporal landscape and the recognition that the pursuit of ethical decision-making may demand a nuanced understanding of the potential consequences of historical interventions.

Conclusion: The Tapestry of Time Unraveling:

As we conclude our exploration of chaos and disruptions in historical events through the lens of time travel, the tapestry of time unravels with profound implications. The intricate interplay between the butterfly effect, historical integrity, temporal paradoxes, unintended consequences, cultural shifts and paradigm changes, and ethical dilemmas defines the landscape where time travelers grapple with the complexities of reshaping the fabric of history. In the chapters that follow, we will continue our journey, exploring additional considerations that shape the frontiers of temporal exploration and redefine our perception of what may be achievable within the dynamic framework of the temporal landscape.

Unintended consequences and the fragility of historical occurrences

In the labyrinth of time travel, the concept of unintended consequences looms as a specter, casting shadows over the landscape of historical impact. This chapter delves into the intricate web of unintended consequences and the fragility of historical occurrences, exploring how the slightest temporal intervention may lead to unforeseen outcomes, altering the course of history in ways both subtle and profound.

The Ripple Effect of Temporal Interference:

At the heart of unintended consequences lies the profound truth that temporal interventions, even with the purest intentions, can set in motion a cascade of changes—a ripple effect that reverberates through time, leaving an indelible mark on the tapestry of history. The exploration begins by unraveling the complexities of the ripple effect, examining how the actions of time travelers may resonate far beyond the initial point of intervention.

Philosophically, the consideration of the ripple effect raises questions about the nature of causality and the potential consequences of even the most well-intentioned actions within the context of historical events. If the ripple effect proves pervasive, the exploration extends to considerations of the philosophical dimensions of agency and the intricate interplay between intentionality and the dynamic framework of the temporal landscape.

Consider a scenario where time travelers, in their attempts to observe or influence historical events, inadvertently set in motion a ripple effect—a scenario that challenges the deterministic view of history and introduces the unpredictable dynamics of temporal intervention. The philosophical inquiry into the ripple effect becomes a reflection on the audacity of navigating the intricacies of causality within the temporal landscape and the recognition that seemingly insignificant actions may carry profound consequences.

Historical Sensitivity: The Butterfly's Wings and the Hurricane of Change:

The butterfly effect, a metaphorical expression of sensitivity to initial conditions, becomes a focal point in understanding the fragility of historical occurrences. Delicate and unpredictable, the butterfly effect posits that the flap of a butterfly's wings in one part of the world could set off a chain of events leading to a hurricane in another—a metaphorical representation of how small actions may have disproportionate and unforeseen consequences.

Philosophically, the exploration of historical sensitivity raises questions about the nature of causality and the potential consequences of seemingly minor actions within the context of historical events. If historical sensitivity proves pervasive, the exploration extends to considerations of the philosophical dimensions of agency and the intricate web of causation that defines the cosmic narrative.

Consider a scenario where time travelers, in their attempts to observe or influence historical events, grapple with the delicate nature of historical sensitivity—a scenario that challenges the deterministic view of history and introduces the complexities of navigating a landscape where small actions may lead to monumental changes. The philosophical inquiry into historical sensitivity becomes a reflection on the audacity of navigating the intricacies of causality within the temporal landscape and the recognition that seemingly insignificant actions may carry profound consequences.

The Tapestry of Unintended Outcomes:

Unintended consequences weave a complex tapestry, where the actions of time travelers may lead to outcomes that defy expectations and challenge the very fabric of historical occurrences. The exploration involves untangling the threads of unintended outcomes, examining how even the most well-intentioned interventions may give rise to consequences that diverge from the intended trajectory.

Philosophically, the consideration of unintended outcomes raises questions about the nature of human agency and the potential consequences of attempting to shape historical events within the context of time travel. If unintended outcomes prove inherent to temporal intervention, the exploration extends to considerations of the philosophical dimensions of agency and the intricate interplay between human intentions and the dynamic framework of the temporal landscape.

Consider a scenario where time travelers, in their attempts to observe or influence historical events, confront the tapestry of unintended outcomes—a scenario that tests the boundaries of human agency within the temporal landscape. The philosophical inquiry into unintended outcomes becomes a reflection on the audacity of navigating the intricacies of human agency within the temporal landscape and the recognition that the pursuit of well-intentioned actions may demand a humility in the face of temporal uncertainties.

Temporal Contingency: Navigating the Unpredictable Pathways of History:

The concept of temporal contingency emerges as a central theme when exploring unintended consequences and the fragility of historical occurrences. Temporal contingency suggests that historical events are contingent upon specific conditions and occurrences, making the precise prediction of outcomes an inherently challenging endeavor.

Philosophically, the exploration of temporal contingency raises questions about the nature of historical determinism and the potential consequences of attempting to navigate the unpredictable pathways of history within the context of time travel. If temporal contingency proves pervasive, the exploration extends to considerations of the philosophical dimensions of determinism and the challenges of navigating the dynamic framework of historical development.

Consider a scenario where time travelers, in their attempts to observe or influence historical events, grapple with the unpredictable pathways of history—a scenario that challenges the notion of historical determinism and introduces the complexities of navigating a landscape where outcomes may be contingent upon myriad factors. The philosophical inquiry into temporal contingency becomes a reflection on the audacity of navigating the intricacies of historical development within the temporal landscape and the recognition that the pursuit of understanding may demand an appreciation for the unpredictable nature of historical occurrences.

Temporal Unpredictability: The Unseen Threads of Historical Tapestry:

Unseen threads weave through the tapestry of history, representing the temporal unpredictability that arises from unintended consequences. The exploration involves considering how the actions of time travelers, even with the best intentions, may introduce threads of unpredictability that alter the course of historical events, creating a rich and complex narrative shaped by the interplay of seen and unseen forces.

Philosophically, the consideration of temporal unpredictability raises questions about the nature of knowledge and the potential consequences of attempting to shape historical events within the context of time travel. If temporal unpredictability proves inherent to temporal intervention, the exploration extends to considerations of the philosophical dimensions of knowledge acquisition and the challenges of navigating the dynamic framework of historical understanding.

Consider a scenario where time travelers, in their attempts to observe or influence historical events, confront the unseen threads of temporal unpredictability—a scenario that tests the foundations of our understanding of history. The philosophical inquiry into temporal unpredictability becomes a reflection on the audacity of acquiring knowledge within the dynamic landscape of the temporal tapestry and the recognition that the pursuit of understanding may demand an acceptance of the inherent unpredictability of historical occurrences.

Ethical Quandaries: The Moral Implications of Unintended Consequences:

The interplay between unintended consequences and ethical dilemmas becomes a focal point when examining the fragility of historical occurrences through time travel. The exploration involves considering how the unforeseen outcomes of temporal interventions may introduce moral quandaries, challenging the ethical responsibilities of those who possess the power to influence the course of history.

Philosophically, the consideration of ethical quandaries raises questions about the nature of moral responsibility and the potential consequences of attempting to shape historical events within the context of time travel. If ethical quandaries prove inherent to temporal intervention, the exploration extends to considerations of the philosophical dimensions of moral decision-making and the challenges of navigating the dynamic framework of ethical responsibility.

Consider a scenario where time travelers, in their attempts to observe or influence historical events, confront profound ethical quandaries—a scenario that tests the boundaries of moral responsibility within the temporal landscape. The philosophical inquiry into ethical quandaries becomes a reflection on the audacity of navigating the intricacies of moral decision-making within the dynamic framework of temporal exploration and the recognition that the pursuit of ethical responsibility may demand a nuanced understanding of the potential consequences of historical interventions.

Conclusion: The Fragility of Threads in the Tapestry of Time:

As we conclude our exploration of unintended consequences and the fragility of historical occurrences through the lens of time travel, the fragility of threads in the tapestry of time becomes apparent. The intricate interplay between the ripple effect, historical sensitivity, unintended outcomes, temporal contingency, temporal unpredictability, and ethical quandaries defines the landscape where time travelers grapple with the complexities of reshaping the fabric of history. In the chapters that follow, we will continue our journey, exploring additional considerations that shape the frontiers of temporal exploration and redefine our perception of what may be achievable within the dynamic framework of the temporal landscape.

Imagining scenarios of historical interference and their implications

The allure of time travel often sparks the imagination to contemplate scenarios where individuals, armed with the ability to traverse temporal landscapes, intervene in historical events. This chapter embarks on a speculative journey, imagining scenarios of historical interference and unraveling the profound implications that may unfold as the fabric of history is woven and rewoven by the hands of time travelers.

Scenario 1: The Altered Outcome of Key Battles:

In this imagined scenario, time travelers set their sights on pivotal battles that shaped the course of civilizations. Consider a world where, through clandestine interventions, battles like Marathon, Waterloo, or Stalingrad take unexpected turns. The implications reverberate through the centuries, reshaping the geopolitical landscape and influencing the trajectory of nations.

Philosophically, the exploration of altered battle outcomes raises questions about the nature of causality and the potential consequences of manipulating key historical events within the context of time travel. If altered battle outcomes prove transformative, the exploration extends to considerations of the philosophical dimensions of agency and the intricate web of causation that defines the cosmic narrative.

Consider a scenario where time travelers, in their attempts to observe or influence historical events, inadvertently alter the outcomes of key battles—a scenario that challenges the deterministic view of history and introduces the complexities of navigating a landscape where the fate of nations hangs in the balance. The philosophical inquiry into altered battle outcomes becomes a reflection on the audacity of navigating the intricacies of causality within the temporal landscape and the recognition that seemingly insignificant actions may carry profound consequences.

Scenario 2: The Meddling in Political Successions:

In this speculative scenario, time travelers delve into the delicate fabric of political successions, altering the ascension of leaders who left an indelible mark on history. Imagine a world where the succession of rulers like Julius Caesar, Elizabeth I, or Lincoln takes unexpected turns. The implications cascade through time, reshaping the ideological underpinnings of nations and influencing the course of political evolution.

Philosophically, the exploration of altered political successions raises questions about the nature of historical determinism and the potential consequences of attempting to navigate the intricate pathways of political development within the context of time travel. If altered successions prove transformative, the exploration extends to considerations of the philosophical dimensions of determinism and the challenges of reshaping the political landscape through temporal intervention.

Consider a scenario where time travelers, in their attempts to observe or influence historical events, inadvertently alter the successions of key political figures—a scenario that tests the boundaries of historical determinism and introduces the complexities of navigating a landscape where the destinies of nations are shaped by the choices of leaders. The philosophical inquiry into altered political successions becomes a reflection on the audacity of navigating the intricacies of determinism within the temporal landscape and the recognition that the pursuit of reshaping political landscapes may demand an appreciation for the unpredictable nature of historical occurrences.

Scenario 3: Cultural Renaissance and the Altered Course of Artistic Movements:

In this imaginative scenario, time travelers turn their attention to cultural renaissances and artistic movements, ushering in waves of creativity that redefine the cultural fabric of societies. Envision a world where interventions lead to the flourishing of artistic movements like the Renaissance, Romanticism, or the Harlem Renaissance in unexpected locations and times. The implications resonate through the annals of creativity, shaping the way societies express themselves and altering the trajectory of cultural evolution.

Philosophically, the exploration of altered artistic movements raises questions about the nature of cultural identity and the potential consequences of attempting to navigate the intricate pathways of artistic expression within the context of time travel. If altered movements prove transformative, the exploration extends to considerations of the philosophical dimensions of cultural evolution and the challenges of reshaping the artistic landscape through temporal intervention.

Consider a scenario where time travelers, in their attempts to observe or influence historical events, inadvertently alter the courses of artistic movements—a scenario that challenges the deterministic view of cultural evolution and introduces the complexities of navigating a landscape where creativity reshapes the cultural identity of societies. The philosophical inquiry into altered artistic movements becomes a reflection on the audacity of navigating the intricacies of cultural evolution within the temporal landscape and the recognition that the pursuit of reshaping artistic landscapes may demand an understanding of the unpredictable nature of historical occurrences.

Scenario 4: Technological Leapfrogging and the Altered Trajectory of Innovation:

In this speculative scenario, time travelers embark on a journey to influence the trajectory of technological innovation, propelling societies to unprecedented heights of advancement. Imagine a world where interventions lead to the acceleration of technological progress during critical junctures like the Industrial Revolution, the Information

Age, or the space race. The implications echo through time, reshaping the way societies harness the power of innovation and altering the course of technological evolution.

Philosophically, the exploration of accelerated technological progress raises questions about the nature of innovation and the potential consequences of attempting to navigate the intricate pathways of technological development within the context of time travel. If accelerated progress proves transformative, the exploration extends to considerations of the philosophical dimensions of technological evolution and the challenges of reshaping the technological landscape through temporal intervention.

Consider a scenario where time travelers, in their attempts to observe or influence historical events, inadvertently accelerate the trajectory of technological innovation—a scenario that challenges the deterministic view of technological evolution and introduces the complexities of navigating a landscape where the power of human ingenuity reshapes the foundations of societies. The philosophical inquiry into accelerated technological progress becomes a reflection on the audacity of navigating the intricacies of technological evolution within the temporal landscape and the recognition that the pursuit of reshaping technological landscapes may demand an understanding of the unpredictable nature of historical occurrences.

Scenario 5: Social Movements and Altered Paths to Equality:

In this imaginative scenario, time travelers delve into the history of social movements and struggles for equality, altering the pathways that led to pivotal moments in the fight against discrimination. Envision a world where interventions contribute to the acceleration of social movements like the Civil Rights Movement, the Suffragette Movement, or LGBTQ+ rights. The implications reverberate through the annals of social progress, reshaping the way societies approach issues of equality and justice.

Philosophically, the exploration of accelerated social progress raises questions about the nature of societal change and the potential consequences of attempting to navigate the intricate pathways of social evolution within the context of time travel. If accelerated progress proves transformative, the exploration extends to considerations of the philosophical dimensions of social evolution and the challenges of reshaping the societal landscape through temporal intervention.

Consider a scenario where time travelers, in their attempts to observe or influence historical events, inadvertently accelerate the trajectories of social movements—a scenario that challenges the deterministic view of societal evolution and introduces the complexities of navigating a landscape where the fight for justice reshapes the foundations of communities. The philosophical inquiry into accelerated social progress becomes a reflection on the audacity of navigating the intricacies of societal evolution within the temporal landscape and the recognition that the pursuit of reshaping societal landscapes may demand an understanding of the unpredictable nature of historical occurrences.

Scenario 6: Environmental Conservation and the Altered Course of Ecological History:

In this speculative scenario, time travelers focus on the challenges of environmental conservation, altering the pathways that led to pivotal moments in the awareness and protection of the planet. Envision a world where interventions contribute to the acceleration of environmental movements like the establishment of national parks, the adoption of sustainable practices, or the global efforts to combat climate change. The implications ripple through the tapestry of ecological history, reshaping the way societies interact with the natural world and altering the course of environmental conservation.

Philosophically, the exploration of accelerated environmental progress raises questions about the nature of human stewardship and the potential consequences of attempting to navigate the intricate pathways of ecological development within the context of time travel. If accelerated progress proves transformative, the exploration extends to considerations of the philosophical dimensions of environmental responsibility and the challenges of reshaping the ecological landscape through temporal intervention.

Consider a scenario where time travelers, in their attempts to observe or influence historical events, inadvertently accelerate the trajectories of environmental movements—a scenario that challenges the deterministic view of ecological evolution and introduces the complexities of navigating a landscape where the preservation of the planet reshapes the foundations of human interaction with the natural world. The philosophical inquiry into accelerated environmental progress becomes a reflection on the audacity of navigating the intricacies of ecological evolution within the temporal landscape and the recognition that the pursuit of reshaping ecological landscapes may demand an understanding of the unpredictable nature of historical occurrences.

Conclusion: The Tapestry of Imagined Scenarios and Uncharted Implications:

As we conclude our journey through imagined scenarios of historical interference and their implications, the tapestry of time reveals the intricate interplay between the actions of time travelers and the unfolding narratives of history. The exploration of altered battle outcomes, political successions, artistic movements, technological innovation, social progress, and environmental conservation highlights the audacity of navigating the complexities of reshaping the fabric of history. In the chapters that follow, we will continue our exploration, delving into additional considerations that shape the frontiers of temporal exploration and redefine our perception of what may be achievable within the dynamic framework of the temporal landscape.

Discussing the potential risks of altering the course of history

In the realm of time travel, the prospect of altering the course of history beckons with tantalizing possibilities. However, beneath the surface of this allure lies a complex tapestry of potential risks, intricately woven into the fabric of temporal manipulation. This chapter delves into the perilous waters of altering history, exploring the myriad risks that may unfold when the past becomes a malleable canvas in the hands of time travelers.

Temporal Butterfly Effect: Unintended Consequences Magnified:

One of the primary risks associated with altering the course of history lies in the temporal butterfly effect—a phenomenon where seemingly insignificant changes may lead to disproportionately significant and unpredictable outcomes. As time travelers intervene in historical events, the ripple effects of their actions may cascade through time, magnifying the impact in ways that defy anticipation.

The exploration of the temporal butterfly effect raises philosophical questions about the nature of causality and the inherent unpredictability of complex systems. The risk of unintended consequences magnified becomes a central concern, highlighting the potential for even well-intentioned interventions to unleash a cascade of events with far-reaching implications.

Consider a scenario where a seemingly minor alteration in a historical event leads to the emergence of an entirely different sociopolitical landscape—a landscape fraught with unforeseen challenges and complexities. The philosophical inquiry into the temporal butterfly effect becomes a reflection on the audacity of navigating the intricacies of causality within the temporal landscape and the recognition that the pursuit of altering history may demand an acute awareness of the potential for unintended consequences.

Paradoxes of Temporal Interference: Navigating the Labyrinth of Contradictions:

Temporal paradoxes, such as the grandfather paradox, pose significant risks when altering the course of history. The grandfather paradox, for instance, suggests that an individual traveling back in time could inadvertently prevent their grandparents from meeting, thus negating their own existence. The labyrinth of contradictions inherent in temporal interference introduces the risk of creating logically incoherent scenarios.

Philosophically, the exploration of temporal paradoxes raises questions about the nature of logic and the potential consequences of attempting to navigate the intricate pathways of time within the context of alteration. If paradoxes prove inherent to temporal intervention, the exploration extends to considerations of the philosophical dimensions of logic and the challenges of reshaping the fabric of history without succumbing to logical inconsistencies.

Consider a scenario where time travelers, in their attempts to observe or influence historical events, grapple with the paradoxes of temporal interference—a scenario that challenges the very foundations of logical reasoning and introduces the complexities of navigating a landscape where contradictions may emerge. The philosophical inquiry into temporal paradoxes becomes a reflection on the audacity of altering history within the dynamic framework of logical constraints and the recognition that the pursuit of reshaping historical landscapes may demand an understanding of the potential contradictions that may arise.

Cultural Dissonance: The Risk of Shattered Identities and Values:

As time travelers intervene in historical events, there is a risk of cultural dissonance—a phenomenon where alterations to key moments may lead to the emergence of divergent cultural identities and values. The risk lies in the potential for societies to evolve along trajectories that foster distinct beliefs, norms, and worldviews, creating a dissonance between the altered and unaltered timelines.

Philosophically, the exploration of cultural dissonance raises questions about the nature of cultural identity and the potential consequences of attempting to navigate the intricate pathways of societal development within the context of time travel. If cultural dissonance proves pervasive, the exploration extends to considerations of the philosophical dimensions of identity and the challenges of reshaping the cultural fabric without eroding the foundations of societal coherence.

Consider a scenario where time travelers, in their attempts to observe or influence historical events, inadvertently foster cultural dissonance—a scenario that challenges the very essence of cultural identity and introduces the complexities of navigating a landscape where societies may evolve along divergent paths. The philosophical inquiry into cultural dissonance becomes a reflection on the audacity of altering history within the dynamic framework of cultural evolution and the recognition that the pursuit of reshaping societal landscapes may demand an understanding of the potential risks to cultural coherence.

Ethical Quandaries: The Moral Implications of Playing with the Past:

The potential risks of altering the course of history extend into the realm of ethical quandaries, as time travelers grapple with the moral implications of their interventions. The risk lies in the ethical responsibility associated with the power to shape the past, as the actions of time travelers may impact the lives of individuals and alter the course of entire civilizations.

Philosophically, the exploration of ethical quandaries raises questions about the nature of moral responsibility and the potential consequences of attempting to navigate the intricate pathways of ethical decision-making within the context of time travel. If ethical quandaries prove inherent to temporal intervention, the exploration extends to considerations of the philosophical dimensions of moral agency and the challenges of reshaping the moral landscape without succumbing to ethical dilemmas.

Consider a scenario where time travelers, in their attempts to observe or influence historical events, confront profound ethical quandaries—a scenario that tests the boundaries of moral responsibility within the temporal landscape. The philosophical inquiry into ethical quandaries becomes a reflection on the audacity of altering history within the dynamic framework of ethical responsibility and the recognition that the pursuit of reshaping ethical landscapes may demand a nuanced understanding of the potential consequences of historical interventions.

Political Turmoil: Upheaval Caused by Manipulating Power Dynamics:

When altering historical events, there is a significant risk of political turmoil, as the manipulation of power dynamics may lead to unpredictable consequences. The risk lies in the potential for interventions to disrupt established political structures, leading to upheaval, conflict, and the emergence of alternative power structures that may be less stable or more prone to authoritarianism.

Philosophically, the exploration of political turmoil raises questions about the nature of political stability and the potential consequences of attempting to navigate the intricate pathways of political development within the context of time travel. If political turmoil proves pervasive, the exploration extends to considerations of the philosophical dimensions of political theory and the challenges of reshaping the political landscape without destabilizing societal structures.

Consider a scenario where time travelers, in their attempts to observe or influence historical events, inadvertently cause political turmoil—a scenario that challenges the stability of political structures and introduces the complexities of navigating a landscape where the balance of power may shift dramatically. The philosophical inquiry into political turmoil becomes a reflection on the audacity of altering history within the dynamic framework of political development and the recognition that the pursuit of reshaping political landscapes may demand an understanding of the potential risks to societal stability.

Conclusion: Navigating the Tempest of Altered Histories and Uncharted Risks:

As we navigate the perilous waters of altering the course of history, the tempest of altered histories and uncharted risks comes into sharp focus. The exploration of the temporal butterfly effect, paradoxes of temporal interference, cultural dissonance, ethical quandaries, and political turmoil highlights the audacity of reshaping the fabric of history. In the chapters that follow, we will continue our journey, delving into additional considerations that shape the frontiers of temporal exploration and redefine our perception of what may be achievable within the dynamic framework of the temporal landscape.

Chapter 5: Human Limitations
Biological constraints on humans attempting time travel

The allure of time travel captivates the human imagination, offering a tantalizing glimpse into the realms of the past and the future. Yet, as we embark on the odyssey of temporal exploration, we must grapple with the inherent biological constraints that shape the very fabric of our existence. This chapter delves into the intricate interplay between the human form and the aspirations of time travelers, exploring the profound challenges posed by biological limitations.

The Fragile Vessel: The Human Body and the Ravages of Temporal Displacement:

At the core of the biological constraints on time travel lies the fragility of the human body in the face of temporal displacement. The act of traversing time demands a profound reshaping of our understanding of physiology, as the human body is subjected to forces and conditions that defy the normative experiences of existence.

Consider the impact of temporal displacement on the cardiovascular system, the respiratory apparatus, and the delicate balance of bodily functions. The acceleration or deceleration of the aging process introduces complexities that extend beyond the superficial concerns of physical appearance, delving into the very essence of cellular and molecular integrity.

Philosophically, the exploration of the fragile vessel raises questions about the nature of corporeal existence and the potential consequences of attempting to navigate the intricate pathways of time within the context of the human form. If the fragility of the human body proves a formidable obstacle, the exploration extends to considerations of the philosophical dimensions of bodily integrity and the challenges of reshaping the fabric of time without succumbing to the ravages of temporal displacement.

Consider a scenario where time travelers, in their attempts to traverse the temporal landscape, confront the fragility of the human vessel—a scenario that challenges the very foundations of bodily integrity and introduces the complexities of navigating a landscape where the forces of time may exact a toll on the corporeal form. The philosophical inquiry into the fragile vessel becomes a reflection on the audacity of navigating the intricacies of corporeal existence within the temporal landscape and the recognition that the pursuit of temporal exploration may demand an acute awareness of the potential consequences to the human body.

The Mind as Temporal Navigator: Cognitive Challenges and the Limitations of Temporal Understanding:

As time travelers embark on the journey through temporal landscapes, the cognitive challenges inherent in understanding and processing temporal phenomena come to the forefront. The mind, tasked with comprehending the non-linear nature of time, faces limitations that extend beyond the conventional boundaries of temporal perception.

Consider the intricacies of memory and the challenges posed by the integration of experiences from altered temporal realities. The non-linear nature of time introduces paradoxes in the fabric of memory, challenging the mind to reconcile divergent timelines and alternate histories. The cognitive dissonance arising from temporal navigation raises questions about the nature of consciousness and the potential consequences of attempting to navigate the intricate pathways of time within the context of the human mind.

Philosophically, the exploration of cognitive challenges raises questions about the nature of consciousness and the potential consequences of attempting to navigate the intricate pathways of time within the context of the human mind. If cognitive challenges prove inherent to temporal navigation, the exploration extends to considerations of the philosophical dimensions of consciousness and the challenges of reshaping the fabric of time without succumbing to the limitations of temporal understanding.

Consider a scenario where time travelers, in their attempts to comprehend and navigate temporal landscapes, grapple with cognitive challenges—a scenario that tests the very foundations of temporal perception and introduces the complexities of navigating a landscape where the mind must confront the inherent limitations of temporal understanding. The philosophical inquiry into cognitive challenges becomes a reflection on the audacity of navigating the intricacies of consciousness within the temporal landscape and the recognition that the pursuit of temporal exploration may demand an understanding of the potential constraints imposed by the human mind.

Temporal Stress and Psychological Strain: The Toll of Unraveling Temporal Mysteries:

Temporal exploration, with its paradoxes, uncertainties, and disruptions to conventional reality, imposes a psychological toll on the individuals undertaking the journey. The very act of unraveling the mysteries of time introduces stressors and strains that extend beyond the normative experiences of psychological well-being.

Consider the impact of temporal stress on mental health, as individuals grapple with the dissonance between the familiar and the unfamiliar, the known and the unknown. The psychological strain of temporal exploration raises questions about the nature of mental resilience and the potential consequences of attempting to navigate the intricate pathways of time within the context of the human psyche.

Philosophically, the exploration of psychological strain raises questions about the nature of mental well-being and the potential consequences of attempting to navigate the intricate pathways of time within the context of the human psyche. If psychological strain proves inherent to temporal exploration, the exploration extends to considerations of the philosophical dimensions of mental resilience and the challenges of reshaping the fabric of time without succumbing to the tolls of psychological strain.

Consider a scenario where time travelers, in their attempts to unravel temporal mysteries, confront psychological strain—a scenario that challenges the very foundations of mental resilience and introduces the complexities of navigating a landscape where the psyche must withstand the stresses imposed by temporal exploration. The philosophical inquiry into psychological strain becomes a reflection on the audacity of navigating the intricacies of mental well-being within the temporal landscape and the recognition that the pursuit of temporal exploration may demand an understanding of the potential tolls on the human psyche.

Temporal Hubris: The Presumption of Mastery Over Time:

At the heart of the biological constraints on time travel lies the notion of temporal hubris—the presumption that humanity can master time itself. The audacious pursuit of temporal exploration, driven by the desire to transcend the limitations of temporal existence, raises questions about the nature of human ambition and the potential consequences of attempting to navigate the intricate pathways of time.

Consider the implications of temporal hubris on the fabric of human identity and the collective psyche. The presumption of mastery over time introduces a narrative where individuals, in their pursuit of temporal transcendence, confront the very essence of what it means to be human. The philosophical inquiry into temporal hubris becomes a reflection on the audacity of navigating the intricacies of temporal existence and the recognition that the pursuit of temporal exploration may demand a humility in the face of the mysteries that time presents.

Consider a scenario where time travelers, in their attempts to master time, grapple with the consequences of temporal hubris—a scenario that challenges the very foundations of human ambition and introduces the complexities of navigating a landscape where the presumption of temporal mastery may lead to unforeseen consequences. The philosophical inquiry into temporal hubris becomes a reflection on the audacity of altering the fabric of time within the dynamic framework of human ambition and the recognition that the pursuit of temporal exploration may demand a humility in the face of the mysteries that time presents.

Conclusion: Navigating the Biological Odyssey with Humility and Awareness:

As we navigate the biological odyssey of time travel, the constraints of the human form come into sharp focus. The exploration of the fragile vessel, cognitive challenges, psychological strain, and temporal hubris highlights the audacity of reshaping the fabric of time. In the chapters that follow, we will continue our journey, delving into additional considerations that shape the frontiers of temporal exploration and redefine our perception of what may be achievable within the dynamic framework of the temporal landscape.

Impact on the human body and mind

As we embark on the exploration of time travel, the intricacies of its impact on the human body and mind come to the forefront. The temporal odyssey, while alluring, presents profound challenges that extend beyond the superficial veneer of adventure. This chapter delves into the unraveling tapestry of the human experience, navigating the complexities of the impact that temporal exploration inflicts on the delicate union of body and mind.

The Physical Toll: Navigating the Ravages of Temporal Displacement on the Human Body:

Temporal displacement, a fundamental aspect of time travel, imposes a physical toll on the human body. As individuals traverse the fabric of time, subjected to forces and conditions that defy conventional understanding, the physiological consequences become apparent. The acceleration or deceleration of the aging process, the distortion of bodily functions, and the challenges of adapting to alternate temporal realities all contribute to the unraveling tapestry of the human physique.

Consider the impact on cardiovascular health, respiratory integrity, and the overall stability of bodily functions. The physical toll of temporal displacement raises questions about the nature of corporeal resilience and the potential consequences of subjecting the human body to the rigors of temporal exploration. If the physical toll proves a formidable obstacle, the exploration extends to considerations of the philosophical dimensions of bodily integrity and the challenges of reshaping the fabric of time without succumbing to the ravages of temporal displacement.

In navigating the physical toll, time travelers must confront scenarios where the very essence of their corporeal existence is subjected to forces that challenge the boundaries of physiological endurance. The philosophical inquiry into the physical toll becomes a reflection on the audacity of navigating the intricacies of corporeal existence within the temporal landscape and the recognition that the pursuit of temporal exploration may demand an acute awareness of the potential consequences to the human body.

Cognitive Dissonance: The Mental Strain of Navigating Non-Linear Temporal Realities:

Temporal exploration introduces cognitive dissonance—a mental strain arising from the attempt to comprehend and navigate non-linear temporal realities. The human mind, accustomed to the linear progression of time, grapples with the paradoxes and uncertainties inherent in traversing the temporal landscape. The integration of experiences from altered temporal realities challenges the fabric of memory, introducing dissonance that extends beyond the normative boundaries of cognitive functioning.

Consider the intricacies of memory integration and the challenges of reconciling divergent timelines. The cognitive dissonance arising from temporal navigation raises questions about the nature of consciousness and the potential consequences of attempting to navigate the intricate pathways of time within the context of the human mind. If cognitive dissonance proves inherent to temporal navigation, the exploration extends to considerations of the philosophical dimensions of consciousness and the challenges of reshaping the fabric of time without succumbing to the limitations of temporal understanding.

In navigating cognitive dissonance, time travelers find themselves in scenarios where the familiar constructs of memory and perception are subjected to forces that challenge the very foundations of cognitive coherence. The philosophical inquiry into cognitive dissonance becomes a reflection on the audacity of navigating the intricacies of consciousness within the temporal landscape and the recognition that the pursuit of temporal exploration may demand an understanding of the potential constraints imposed by the human mind.

Psychological Strain: The Toll of Unraveling Temporal Mysteries on Mental Well-Being:

Temporal exploration imposes a psychological strain on individuals unraveling the mysteries of time. The act of navigating the temporal landscape, with its paradoxes, uncertainties, and disruptions to conventional reality, introduces stressors and strains that extend beyond the normative experiences of psychological well-being. The psyche, subjected to the dissonance between the known and the unknown, faces challenges that transcend the superficial allure of temporal adventure.

Consider the impact of temporal stress on mental health and the toll of unraveling temporal mysteries on overall psychological well-being. The psychological strain of temporal exploration raises questions about the nature of mental resilience and the potential consequences of attempting to navigate the intricate pathways of time within the context of the human psyche. If psychological strain proves inherent to temporal exploration, the exploration extends to considerations of the philosophical dimensions of mental resilience and the challenges of reshaping the fabric of time without succumbing to the tolls of psychological strain.

In navigating psychological strain, time travelers confront scenarios where the very essence of their mental well-being is subjected to forces that challenge the boundaries of psychological resilience. The philosophical inquiry into psychological strain becomes a reflection on the audacity of navigating the intricacies of mental well-being within the temporal landscape and the recognition that the pursuit of temporal exploration may demand an understanding of the potential tolls on the human psyche.

Temporal Hubris Revisited: The Presumption of Mastery Over Body and Mind:

At the core of the impact on the human body and mind lies the notion of temporal hubris—the presumption that humanity can master not only time itself but also the profound interplay between body and mind within the temporal landscape. The audacious pursuit of temporal exploration, driven by the desire to transcend the limitations of temporal existence, raises questions about the nature of human ambition and the potential consequences of attempting to navigate the intricate pathways of time.

Consider the implications of temporal hubris on the fabric of human identity and the collective psyche. The presumption of mastery over both body and mind introduces a narrative where individuals, in their pursuit of temporal transcendence, confront the very essence of what it means to be human. The philosophical inquiry into temporal hubris becomes a reflection on the audacity of navigating the intricacies of temporal existence and the recognition that the pursuit of temporal exploration may demand a humility in the face of the mysteries that time presents.

In revisiting temporal hubris, time travelers find themselves in scenarios where the very essence of their humanity is subjected to forces that challenge the boundaries of bodily and mental mastery. The philosophical inquiry into temporal hubris becomes a reflection on the audacity of altering the fabric of time within the dynamic framework of human ambition and the recognition that the pursuit of temporal exploration may demand a humility in the face of the mysteries that time presents.

Conclusion: Navigating the Impact on Body and Mind with Humility and Awareness:

As we navigate the impact of time travel on the fragile union of body and mind, the complexities of unraveling the tapestry of the human experience come into sharp focus. The exploration of the physical toll, cognitive dissonance, psychological strain, and temporal hubris highlights the audacity of reshaping the fabric of time. In the chapters that follow, we will continue our journey, delving into additional considerations that shape the frontiers of temporal exploration and redefine our perception of what may be achievable within the dynamic framework of the temporal landscape.

Psychological challenges associated with time travel

In the pursuit of time travel, beyond the tangible hurdles lie the intangible, yet profound, psychological challenges that confront individuals daring to tread the temporal landscape. This chapter delves into the intricate web of psychological complexities associated with time travel, exploring the depths of the human psyche as it grapples with the paradoxes, uncertainties, and disruptions inherent in temporal exploration.

The Temporal Paradox: A Mind-Bending Conundrum:

At the heart of the psychological challenges associated with time travel lies the temporal paradox—a mind-bending conundrum that challenges the very fabric of logical reasoning. The paradoxes, such as the grandfather paradox, where the actions of a time traveler could prevent their own existence, introduce cognitive dissonance that defies conventional understanding.

Consider the mental strain of reconciling divergent timelines, where cause and effect become intertwined in a complex dance. The temporal paradox raises questions about the nature of logic and the potential consequences of attempting to navigate the intricate pathways of time within the context of the human mind. If the temporal paradox proves to be an insurmountable hurdle, the exploration extends to considerations of the philosophical dimensions of logical coherence and the challenges of reshaping the fabric of time without succumbing to the labyrinth of paradox.

In navigating the temporal paradox, time travelers find themselves in scenarios where the very essence of their cognitive coherence is subjected to forces that challenge the foundations of logical reasoning. The philosophical inquiry into the temporal paradox becomes a reflection on the audacity of navigating the intricacies of consciousness within the temporal landscape and the recognition that the pursuit of temporal exploration may demand an understanding of the potential contradictions that may arise.

The Shifting Sands of Reality: Coping with Altered Perceptions:

Temporal exploration, by its very nature, alters perceptions of reality. As individuals traverse the temporal landscape, they are confronted with alternate versions of events, divergent timelines, and a kaleidoscope of possibilities. The shifting sands of reality introduce challenges to the human mind, as it must adapt to a dynamic environment where the foundations of perception are in constant flux.

Consider the mental strain of adapting to the fluid nature of reality, where the certainties of the past and the possibilities of the future merge and diverge. The shifting sands of reality raise questions about the nature of perception and the potential consequences of attempting to navigate the intricate pathways of time within the context of the human mind. If the fluidity of reality proves to be a psychological obstacle, the exploration extends to considerations of the philosophical dimensions of perception and the challenges of reshaping the fabric of time without succumbing to the disorientation induced by shifting realities.

In navigating the shifting sands of reality, time travelers confront scenarios where the very essence of their perceptual framework is subjected to forces that challenge the boundaries of cognitive adaptation. The philosophical inquiry into the shifting sands of reality becomes a reflection on the audacity of navigating the intricacies of consciousness within the temporal landscape and the recognition that the pursuit of temporal exploration may demand an understanding of the potential shifts in perception that may occur.

Existential Angst: Wrestling with the Nature of Being and Becoming:

Temporal exploration thrusts individuals into the throes of existential angst—a profound wrestling with the nature of being and becoming. As time travelers grapple with the implications of altering past events or glimpsing into the future, questions about identity, purpose, and the meaning of existence become central to the psychological landscape.

Consider the mental strain of confronting alternate versions of oneself, divergent life paths, and the malleability of destiny. Existential angst raises questions about the nature of identity and the potential consequences of attempting to navigate the intricate pathways of time within the context of the human mind. If existential angst proves to be a psychological burden, the exploration extends to considerations of the philosophical dimensions of identity and the challenges of reshaping the fabric of time without succumbing to the existential quandaries induced by temporal exploration.

In navigating existential angst, time travelers find themselves in scenarios where the very essence of their existential understanding is subjected to forces that challenge the foundations of identity. The philosophical inquiry into existential angst becomes a reflection on the audacity of navigating the intricacies of consciousness within the temporal landscape and the recognition that the pursuit of temporal exploration may demand an understanding of the potential existential quandaries that may arise.

Temporal Isolation: The Loneliness of the Time Traveler:

Temporal exploration, by its solitary nature, introduces a sense of temporal isolation—a loneliness that permeates the psyche of the time traveler. As individuals navigate the temporal landscape, they may find themselves disconnected from the familiar bonds of community, family, and societal structures. The temporal isolation introduces psychological challenges related to the inherent solitude of the temporal journey.

Consider the mental strain of traversing time without the comforting presence of shared experiences, common narratives, and a sense of belonging. Temporal isolation raises questions about the nature of human connection and the potential consequences of attempting to navigate the intricate pathways of time within the context of the human mind. If temporal isolation proves to be a psychological hardship, the exploration extends to considerations of the philosophical dimensions of human connection and the challenges of reshaping the fabric of time without succumbing to the isolation induced by temporal exploration.

In navigating temporal isolation, time travelers confront scenarios where the very essence of their psychological well-being is subjected to forces that challenge the foundations of human connection. The philosophical inquiry into temporal isolation becomes a reflection on the audacity of navigating the intricacies of consciousness within the temporal landscape and the recognition that the pursuit of temporal exploration may demand an understanding of the potential psychological hardships induced by isolation.

Temporal Trauma: The Lingering Scars of Altered Histories:

Temporal exploration may leave individuals grappling with temporal trauma—a psychological condition arising from the exposure to altered histories, traumatic events, or the consequences of interventions in the temporal landscape. The lingering scars of temporal trauma introduce challenges related to mental health, coping mechanisms, and the psychological toll of witnessing or participating in historical alterations.

Consider the mental strain of processing traumatic events, witnessing unintended consequences, or grappling with the ethical implications of temporal interventions. Temporal trauma raises questions about the nature of psychological resilience and the potential consequences of attempting to navigate the intricate pathways of time within the context of the human mind. If temporal trauma proves to be a psychological burden, the exploration extends to considerations of the philosophical dimensions of mental health and the challenges of reshaping the fabric of time without succumbing to the traumatic aftermath induced by temporal exploration.

In navigating temporal trauma, time travelers find themselves in scenarios where the very essence of their psychological well-being is subjected to forces that challenge the foundations of mental resilience. The philosophical inquiry into temporal trauma becomes a reflection on the audacity of navigating the intricacies of consciousness within the temporal landscape and the recognition that the pursuit of temporal exploration may demand an understanding of the potential psychological tolls induced by traumatic experiences.

Conclusion: Navigating the Abyss of Psychological Challenges with Resilience and Awareness:

As we navigate the psychological challenges of temporal exploration, the depths of the human psyche come into sharp focus. The exploration of the temporal paradox, shifting sands of reality, existential angst, temporal isolation, and temporal trauma highlights the audacity of reshaping the fabric of time. In the chapters that follow, we will continue our journey, delving into additional considerations that shape the frontiers of temporal exploration and redefine our perception of what may be achievable within the dynamic framework of the temporal landscape.

Addressing the impracticality of human involvement in time-travel scenarios

As we venture into the heart of time-travel scenarios, the realization dawns that the practicality of human involvement in such endeavors may be far more elusive than the tantalizing prospect of temporal exploration suggests. This chapter delves into the impracticalities that cast a shadow over the human aspiration to traverse the corridors of time, exploring the physical, technological, and existential barriers that challenge the very essence of human involvement in time-travel scenarios.

The Physiological Quandary: The Human Form in the Face of Temporal Displacement:

At the forefront of the impracticalities lies the physiological quandary—the profound challenge posed by the human form when subjected to the rigors of temporal displacement. The very act of traversing time demands a reconsideration of the fundamental aspects of human physiology, as the body grapples with forces that defy the normative experiences of existence.

Consider the impact on cardiovascular health, respiratory integrity, and the overall stability of bodily functions. The physiological quandary raises questions about the nature of corporeal resilience and the potential consequences of subjecting the human body to the relentless demands of temporal exploration. If the physiological quandary proves insurmountable, the exploration extends to considerations of the philosophical dimensions of bodily integrity and the challenges of reshaping the fabric of time without succumbing to the inherent vulnerabilities of the human form.

In addressing the impracticality of human involvement in time-travel scenarios, individuals find themselves confronted with scenarios where the very essence of their corporeal existence is subjected to forces that challenge the boundaries of physiological endurance. The philosophical inquiry into the physiological quandary becomes a reflection on the audacity of navigating the intricacies of corporeal existence within the temporal landscape and the recognition that the pursuit of temporal exploration may demand an acute awareness of the potential consequences to the human body.

Technological Barriers: The Gargantuan Challenge of Crafting Temporal Portals:

Temporal exploration is not solely bound by the limitations of the human form but is equally tethered to the gargantuan challenge of crafting the very portals through which time travel becomes possible. Technological barriers stand as formidable sentinels, demanding an unprecedented leap in human ingenuity, scientific understanding, and engineering prowess to breach the fabric of temporal reality.

Consider the complexities of manipulating the fabric of time itself—crafting portals that can withstand the forces of temporal displacement, navigate the intricacies of causality, and enable safe passage through the corridors of history. Technological barriers raise questions about the nature of human innovation and the potential consequences of attempting to engineer the very framework of temporal reality. If technological barriers prove insurmountable, the exploration extends to considerations of the philosophical dimensions of scientific ambition and the challenges of reshaping the fabric of time without succumbing to the limitations of technological capability.

In grappling with technological barriers, individuals find themselves faced with scenarios where the very essence of their scientific ambition is subjected to forces that challenge the boundaries of technological capability. The philosophical inquiry into technological barriers becomes a reflection on the audacity of navigating the intricacies of scientific innovation within the temporal landscape and the recognition that the pursuit of temporal exploration may demand a profound understanding of the potential limitations of technological endeavors.

Existential Considerations: The Ethical and Moral Quandaries of Time Travel:

Beyond the physiological and technological challenges lie existential considerations—the ethical and moral quandaries that cast a long shadow over the notion of human involvement in time-travel scenarios. Temporal exploration introduces a myriad of ethical dilemmas, questioning the very fabric of human responsibility and accountability in the face of the vast unknown.

Consider the implications of altering historical events, intervening in the course of human affairs, or even inadvertently causing harm to the fabric of time itself. Existential considerations raise questions about the nature of human ethics and the potential consequences of attempting to navigate the intricate pathways of time within the context of moral responsibility. If existential considerations prove insurmountable, the exploration extends to considerations of the philosophical dimensions of moral accountability and the challenges of reshaping the fabric of time without succumbing to the inherent ethical dilemmas of temporal exploration.

In addressing existential considerations, individuals find themselves confronted with scenarios where the very essence of their moral responsibility is subjected to forces that challenge the boundaries of ethical conduct. The philosophical inquiry into existential considerations becomes a reflection on the audacity of navigating the intricacies of moral responsibility within the temporal landscape and the recognition that the pursuit of temporal exploration may demand an acute awareness of the potential ethical dilemmas that may arise.

Temporal Fragility: The Unpredictability of Altered Timelines:

Impracticalities arise not only from the challenges of the human form, technological barriers, and ethical considerations but also from the inherent fragility of altered timelines. The unpredictability of the temporal landscape introduces an element of chaos, as the repercussions of even seemingly minor interventions may cascade into unforeseen and uncontrollable consequences.

Consider the implications of altering historical events or even attempting to "fix" perceived errors in the fabric of time. Temporal fragility raises questions about the nature of unintended consequences and the potential fallout of attempting to navigate the intricate pathways of time without succumbing to the unpredictable nature of altered timelines. If temporal fragility proves insurmountable, the exploration extends to considerations of the philosophical dimensions of temporal consequence and the challenges of reshaping the fabric of time without succumbing to the inherent chaos of altered realities.

In addressing temporal fragility, individuals find themselves confronted with scenarios where the very essence of their temporal interventions is subjected to forces that challenge the boundaries of predictability. The philosophical inquiry into temporal fragility becomes a reflection on the audacity of navigating the intricacies of temporal consequence within the temporal landscape and the recognition that the pursuit of temporal exploration may demand an acute awareness of the potential chaos that may arise.

Conclusion: Navigating the Impracticalities with Humility and Awareness:

As we confront the impracticalities of human involvement in time-travel scenarios, the complexities of the physiological quandary, technological barriers, existential considerations, and temporal fragility come into sharp focus. The exploration of these challenges highlights the audacity of reshaping the fabric of time. In the chapters that follow, we will continue our journey, delving into additional considerations that shape the frontiers of temporal exploration and redefine our perception of what may be achievable within the dynamic framework of the temporal landscape.

Chapter 6: Alternative Perspectives
Dissenting opinions within the scientific and philosophical communities

As we traverse the landscape of time travel, it becomes evident that dissenting opinions within the scientific and philosophical communities weave an intricate tapestry of alternate perspectives. This chapter embarks on a journey into the realms of skepticism, exploring the voices that challenge the mainstream views, proposing alternative theories, and presenting dissenting opinions that challenge the very foundations of the prevailing discourse on temporal exploration.

The Skeptical Pioneers: Champions of Temporal Realism:

Amidst the fervor of temporal exploration, a cadre of skeptical pioneers emerges as champions of temporal realism. These individuals, often rooted in the scientific community, scrutinize the very foundations of time travel theories and present counterarguments that challenge the prevailing optimism surrounding the possibility of traversing the corridors of time.

Consider the arguments rooted in the principles of relativity, quantum mechanics, and the broader landscape of theoretical physics. Skeptical pioneers question the feasibility of manipulating time, pointing to the intricacies of established scientific frameworks that may render temporal travel impractical or even impossible. As we navigate the dissenting opinions, it becomes evident that these skeptical voices provide a counterbalance, urging caution and critical evaluation in the face of temporal enthusiasm.

In exploring dissenting opinions within the scientific and philosophical communities, individuals find themselves confronted with scenarios where the very essence of their temporal aspirations is subjected to the critical scrutiny of skeptical pioneers. The philosophical inquiry into skeptical perspectives becomes a reflection on the audacity of navigating the intricacies of temporal exploration within the scientific landscape and the recognition that dissenting voices play a crucial role in shaping a balanced discourse.

Quantum Skepticism: Navigating Uncertainties in the Fabric of Reality:

Within the realm of dissenting opinions, a notable strand emerges from the field of quantum skepticism—a perspective that questions the very nature of reality and the uncertainties embedded in the fabric of the quantum realm. Quantum skeptics challenge the assumptions that underpin time travel theories, pointing to the inherent uncertainties and probabilistic nature of quantum phenomena.

Consider the debates surrounding the observer effect, quantum entanglement, and the implications of non-locality on the feasibility of manipulating time. Quantum skeptics contend that the very uncertainties that define the quantum world may impose insurmountable challenges to the precision and control required for successful temporal navigation. As we navigate these dissenting perspectives, it becomes evident that the quantum realm introduces complexities that may reshape our understanding of the temporal landscape.

In exploring dissenting opinions within the scientific and philosophical communities, individuals find themselves confronted with scenarios where the very essence of their temporal theories is subjected to the unpredictable nature of quantum skepticism. The philosophical inquiry into quantum perspectives becomes a reflection on the audacity of navigating the intricacies of temporal exploration within the quantum realm and the recognition that dissenting voices from the quantum frontier may redefine the contours of our temporal aspirations.

Temporal Paradox Advocates: Embracing the Complexity of Non-Linear Realities:

As dissenting opinions gain momentum, a unique perspective emerges from the ranks of temporal paradox advocates—individuals who embrace the complexity of non-linear realities and argue that paradoxes may not be insurmountable obstacles but rather gateways to deeper understanding. Temporal paradox advocates challenge the conventional view that paradoxes render time travel untenable, suggesting that these apparent contradictions may hold the key to unlocking the mysteries of temporal navigation.

Consider the arguments surrounding closed timelike curves, self-consistency principles, and the potential resolution of paradoxes within a broader framework of understanding. Temporal paradox advocates contend that, rather than dismissing paradoxes, we should explore them as clues that may lead to a more nuanced comprehension of the temporal fabric. As we navigate these dissenting perspectives, it becomes evident that temporal paradox advocates advocate for a reevaluation of our preconceived notions about the limitations of time travel.

In exploring dissenting opinions within the scientific and philosophical communities, individuals find themselves confronted with scenarios where the very essence of their temporal theories is subjected to the transformative potential of embracing paradoxical realities. The philosophical inquiry into paradox advocacy becomes a reflection on the audacity of navigating the intricacies of temporal exploration within the paradoxical landscape and the recognition that dissenting voices from this perspective may challenge the boundaries of our temporal understanding.

The Philosophical Mavericks: Exploring Time as a Construct of Consciousness:

Within the landscape of dissenting opinions, a cadre of philosophical mavericks explores the notion that time may be a construct of consciousness—a perspective that challenges the conventional understanding of time as an objective and independent entity. Philosophical mavericks question the very foundations of temporal theories, proposing that time, rather than being an external framework, may emerge from the intricacies of subjective experience.

Consider the arguments that delve into the nature of consciousness, subjective temporality, and the potential relativity of time perception. Philosophical mavericks contend that our conventional understanding of time as an external, universal constant may be a conceptual limitation, and exploring consciousness may offer new insights into the dynamics of temporal experience. As we navigate these dissenting perspectives, it becomes evident that philosophical mavericks advocate for a broader, more inclusive view of time that transcends traditional boundaries.

In exploring dissenting opinions within the scientific and philosophical communities, individuals find themselves confronted with scenarios where the very essence of their temporal theories is subjected to the expansive horizons of philosophical mavericks. The philosophical inquiry into consciousness-centric perspectives becomes a reflection on the audacity of navigating the intricacies of temporal exploration within the philosophical landscape and the recognition that dissenting voices from this vantage point may enrich our understanding of the interplay between time and consciousness.

Temporal Pluralism: Embracing Diverse Perspectives in the Tapestry of Time:

As we navigate dissenting opinions within the scientific and philosophical communities, a broader perspective emerges—temporal pluralism, an approach that advocates for embracing diverse viewpoints and acknowledging the complexity of the temporal landscape. Temporal pluralism contends that the richness of our understanding lies in the coexistence of varied theories, dissenting opinions, and alternative perspectives that collectively contribute to the tapestry of temporal exploration.

Consider the arguments in favor of fostering an inclusive discourse that incorporates insights from skepticism, quantum perspectives, paradox advocacy, and consciousness-centric views. Temporal pluralism argues that, rather than seeking a singular, definitive answer, we should celebrate the diversity of thought within the scientific and philosophical communities. As we navigate these dissenting perspectives, it becomes evident that temporal pluralism encourages an open-minded exploration of the multifaceted nature of time.

In exploring dissenting opinions within the scientific and philosophical communities, individuals find themselves confronted with scenarios where the very essence of their temporal theories is subjected to the tapestry of temporal pluralism. The philosophical inquiry into pluralistic perspectives becomes a reflection on the audacity of navigating the intricacies of temporal exploration within a landscape that celebrates the richness of diverse viewpoints and dissenting opinions.

Conclusion: Navigating the Tapestry of Dissent with Intellectual Curiosity and Open-Mindedness:

As we delve into dissenting opinions within the scientific and philosophical communities, the voices of skeptical pioneers, quantum skeptics, temporal paradox advocates, philosophical mavericks, and proponents of temporal pluralism resonate. The exploration of these perspectives highlights the audacity of reshaping the fabric of time. In the chapters that follow, we will continue our journey, delving into additional considerations that shape the frontiers of temporal exploration and redefine our perception of what may be achievable within the dynamic framework of the temporal landscape.

Exploring unconventional theories challenging mainstream views

In the quest to unravel the mysteries of time, unconventional theories emerge as intrepid voyagers challenging the very foundations of mainstream views on temporal exploration. This chapter embarks on a journey into uncharted territories, exploring theories that defy convention, question established paradigms, and beckon us to reconsider the nature of time itself.

Time as a Fluid Construct: Riding the Waves of Chronological Flexibility:

At the forefront of unconventional theories lies the proposition that time is not a rigid, linear construct but rather a fluid entity, subject to dynamic shifts and undulations. Advocates of this perspective suggest that time possesses an inherent flexibility, allowing for the possibility of traversing its currents in ways that challenge our conventional understanding.

Consider the analogy of time as a river, with events flowing along its course. Proponents of fluid time argue that manipulating the currents, altering the course of events, and even navigating against the flow may be conceivable under certain conditions. As we delve into this unconventional theory, it becomes evident that proponents of fluid time challenge us to envision temporal landscapes where the boundaries between past, present, and future blur into a seamless continuum.

In exploring unconventional theories challenging mainstream views, individuals find themselves confronted with scenarios where the very essence of their temporal understanding is subjected to the dynamic currents of fluid time. The philosophical inquiry into this unconventional perspective becomes a reflection on the audacity of navigating the intricacies of temporal exploration within a framework that envisions time as a malleable and fluid entity, transcending the limitations of our conventional perceptions.

Temporal Anomalies: Glimpses into Disruptions Across the Temporal Fabric:

Unconventional theories beckon us to consider the possibility of temporal anomalies—disruptions and irregularities that punctuate the fabric of time. Advocates of this perspective propose that these anomalies may serve as gateways, allowing for brief glimpses into alternate timelines, historical epochs, or even future trajectories.

Consider the concept of a temporal anomaly as a localized disturbance in the temporal fabric, creating windows into different temporal realities. Proponents of this theory suggest that these anomalies may occur naturally or could be artificially induced, providing avenues for temporal exploration. As we navigate this unconventional theory, it becomes evident that advocates of temporal anomalies challenge us to envision a tapestry of time woven with intricate disruptions, each offering a portal to unexplored temporal realms.

In exploring unconventional theories challenging mainstream views, individuals find themselves confronted with scenarios where the very essence of their temporal understanding is subjected to the enigmatic nature of temporal anomalies. The philosophical inquiry into this unconventional perspective becomes a reflection on the audacity of navigating the intricacies of temporal exploration within a framework that embraces disruptions in the fabric of time, inviting us to consider the possibilities of glimpsing beyond the veil of chronological continuity.

Multidimensional Time: Navigating Beyond the Linear Temporal Axis:

Unconventional theories beckon us to venture beyond the constraints of a linear temporal axis and consider the prospect of multidimensional time. Advocates of this perspective propose that time, rather than flowing along a single continuum, exists across multiple dimensions, each offering unique pathways for exploration.

Consider the analogy of time as a tapestry woven with threads representing different dimensions. Proponents of multidimensional time argue that these dimensions coexist, intersect, and diverge, providing avenues for temporal navigation that transcend the limitations of linear progression. As we delve into this unconventional theory, it becomes evident that advocates of multidimensional time challenge us to envision a temporal landscape where alternate realities and divergent timelines converge in a complex dance.

In exploring unconventional theories challenging mainstream views, individuals find themselves confronted with scenarios where the very essence of their temporal understanding is subjected to the multidimensional nature of time. The philosophical inquiry into this unconventional perspective becomes a reflection on the audacity of navigating the intricacies of temporal exploration within a framework that transcends the linear constraints of our conventional perceptions.

Chronicles of Time Travelers: Echoes from Future Expeditions:

Unconventional theories beckon us to consider the possibility that time travelers from the future may already be among us, leaving subtle echoes or imprints of their presence. Advocates of this perspective propose that these temporal pioneers, equipped with advanced technology or consciousness-altering capabilities, may be subtly influencing our timeline, leaving clues that defy conventional explanations.

Consider the notion that anomalies in historical records, unexplained phenomena, or even cultural shifts could be attributed to the interventions of time travelers from the future. Proponents of this theory suggest that these interventions may be intentional, accidental, or even subtle nudges designed to guide the course of history. As we navigate this unconventional theory, it becomes evident that advocates of chronicles of time travelers challenge us to consider the prospect that echoes from future expeditions may already be imprinted on the canvas of our reality.

In exploring unconventional theories challenging mainstream views, individuals find themselves confronted with scenarios where the very essence of their temporal understanding is subjected to the subtle influences of future time travelers. The philosophical inquiry into this unconventional perspective becomes a reflection on the audacity of navigating the intricacies of temporal exploration within a framework that envisions our reality as a canvas subtly shaped by echoes from future expeditions.

Temporal Resonance: Harmonizing with the Vibrations of Past and Future:

Unconventional theories beckon us to explore the concept of temporal resonance—a perspective that suggests individuals or objects may resonate with specific temporal frequencies, allowing for a harmonious connection with events from the past or future. Advocates of this theory propose that resonance, akin to tuning into a frequency, could facilitate a form of temporal communication or interaction.

Consider the idea that certain individuals, places, or artifacts may carry resonances that align with particular moments in time. Proponents of temporal resonance argue that, under the right conditions, individuals could attune themselves to these frequencies, opening channels for communication or even exploration across temporal boundaries. As we delve into this unconventional theory, it becomes evident that advocates of temporal resonance challenge us to consider the possibility of harmonizing with the vibrational echoes of past and future epochs.

In exploring unconventional theories challenging mainstream views, individuals find themselves confronted with scenarios where the very essence of their temporal understanding is subjected to the harmonious frequencies of temporal resonance. The philosophical inquiry into this unconventional perspective becomes a reflection on the audacity of navigating the intricacies of temporal exploration within a framework that envisions resonance as a gateway to the temporal landscapes of the past and future.

Conclusion: Navigating the Uncharted Realms with Open Minds and Imaginative Curiosity:

As we navigate the uncharted realms of unconventional theories challenging mainstream views, the perspectives of fluid time, temporal anomalies, multidimensional time, chronicles of time travelers, and temporal resonance resonate. The exploration of these unconventional theories highlights the audacity of reshaping the fabric of time. In the chapters that follow, we will continue our journey, delving into additional considerations that shape the frontiers of temporal exploration and redefine our perception of what may be achievable within the dynamic framework of the temporal landscape.

Speculative, non-standard perspectives on the nature of time

In our quest to unravel the mysteries of time, we encounter speculative, non-standard perspectives that challenge the very essence of conventional understanding. This chapter ventures into uncharted territories, exploring theories that transcend traditional frameworks and beckon us to consider time through unconventional lenses.

Time as a Cosmic Symphony: Harmonizing the Threads of Existence:

At the forefront of non-standard perspectives lies the notion that time is not merely a linear progression but rather a cosmic symphony—a harmonious interplay of threads weaving the tapestry of existence. Advocates of this perspective propose that events, rather than unfolding along a predetermined path, resonate with one another, creating a symphony of interconnected moments.

Consider the analogy of time as a symphony where each note represents a unique event. Proponents of the cosmic symphony argue that these events, while distinct, contribute to the overall harmony of existence. As we delve into this non-standard perspective, it becomes evident that advocates of the cosmic symphony challenge us to envision time as a dynamic and interconnected expression, transcending the limitations of linear progression.

In exploring non-standard perspectives on the nature of time, individuals find themselves confronted with

scenarios where the very essence of their temporal understanding is subjected to the harmonious threads of the cosmic symphony. The philosophical inquiry into this speculative perspective becomes a reflection on the audacity of navigating the intricacies of temporal exploration within a framework that envisions time as a grand symphony, each moment contributing to the sublime composition of existence.

Time as an Emergent Phenomenon: Unraveling the Mysteries of Temporal Genesis:

Non-standard perspectives beckon us to consider the possibility that time is not a pre-existing framework but rather an emergent phenomenon—an aspect of reality that unfolds and evolves as a consequence of deeper cosmic processes. Advocates of this perspective propose that time, rather than being a fundamental constant, emerges from the complex interplay of fundamental forces.

Consider the idea that time is a product of cosmic evolution, much like galaxies, stars, and planets. Proponents of emergent time argue that the unfolding of the cosmos gives rise to the very concept of temporal progression. As we navigate this non-standard perspective, it becomes evident that advocates of emergent time challenge us to envision a reality where time itself is a dynamic and evolving phenomenon.

In exploring non-standard perspectives on the nature of time, individuals find themselves confronted with

scenarios where the very essence of their temporal understanding is subjected to the emergent nature of temporal genesis. The philosophical inquiry into this speculative perspective becomes a reflection on the audacity of navigating the intricacies of temporal exploration within a framework that envisions time as an emergent phenomenon, intricately woven into the fabric of cosmic evolution.

Time as a Multidimensional Mosaic: Embracing the Complexity of Temporal Dimensions:

Non-standard perspectives beckon us to transcend the constraints of a linear temporal axis and consider the possibility that time is a multidimensional mosaic—a complex interplay of dimensions, each contributing to the richness of temporal experience. Advocates of this perspective propose that our conventional understanding of time as a single, unidirectional flow may be an oversimplification.

Consider the analogy of time as a mosaic where different dimensions represent unique facets of temporal reality. Proponents of the multidimensional mosaic argue that these dimensions coexist, intersect, and influence one another, creating a tapestry of temporal intricacies. As we delve into this non-standard perspective, it becomes evident that advocates of the multidimensional mosaic challenge us to envision a reality where time unfolds along a myriad of interconnected dimensions.

In exploring non-standard perspectives on the nature of time, individuals find themselves confronted with scenarios where the very essence of their temporal understanding is subjected to the complexity of the multidimensional mosaic. The philosophical inquiry into this speculative perspective becomes a reflection on the audacity of navigating the intricacies of temporal exploration within a framework that transcends the linear constraints of our conventional perceptions.

Time as Information: Decoding the Quantum Tapestry of Reality:

Non-standard perspectives beckon us to explore the idea that time is not a fundamental aspect of reality but rather a form of information—an intricate code woven into the quantum fabric of existence. Advocates of this perspective propose that the nature of time is intimately linked to the underlying informational structure of the universe.

Consider the notion that time is akin to a quantum tapestry where information, encoded in the quantum states of particles, unfolds the narrative of reality. Proponents of time as information argue that understanding the quantum nature of reality is key to deciphering the mysteries of temporal progression. As we navigate this non-standard perspective, it becomes evident that advocates of time as information challenge us to envision a reality where time is a quantum code, waiting to be decoded.

In exploring non-standard perspectives on the nature of time, individuals find themselves confronted with scenarios where the very essence of their temporal understanding is subjected to the quantum tapestry of information. The philosophical inquiry into this speculative perspective becomes a reflection on the audacity of navigating the intricacies of temporal exploration within a framework that envisions time as an intricate code embedded in the quantum fabric of reality.

Time as a Simulation: Unveiling the Illusory Nature of Temporal Reality:

Non-standard perspectives beckon us to entertain the possibility that time is not a fundamental aspect of reality but rather a simulation—an illusory construct that shapes our perception of temporal progression. Advocates of this perspective propose that our experience of time may be akin to navigating a meticulously crafted virtual reality.

Consider the idea that time is a simulated construct where our consciousness interacts with a sophisticated temporal framework. Proponents of time as a simulation argue that the very nature of our temporal experience may be a product of a higher-dimensional simulation. As we delve into this non-standard perspective, it becomes evident that advocates of time as a simulation challenge us to question the authenticity of our temporal reality.

In exploring non-standard perspectives on the nature of time, individuals find themselves confronted with

scenarios where the very essence of their temporal understanding is subjected to the illusory nature of temporal simulation. The philosophical inquiry into this speculative perspective becomes a reflection on the audacity of navigating the intricacies of temporal exploration within a framework that envisions time as a virtual construct, inviting us to question the boundaries of our temporal perceptions.

Conclusion: Navigating the Speculative Frontiers with Intellectual Curiosity and Open-Mindedness:

As we navigate the speculative frontiers of non-standard perspectives challenging conventional views, the perspectives of the cosmic symphony, emergent time, multidimensional mosaic, time as information, and temporal simulation resonate. The exploration of these speculative perspectives highlights the audacity of reshaping the fabric of time. In the chapters that follow, we will continue our journey, delving into additional considerations that shape the frontiers of temporal exploration and redefine our perception of what may be achievable within the dynamic framework of the temporal landscape.

Examining the diversity of thought on the possibility of time travel

In the vast landscape of temporal exploration, diverse perspectives emerge, shaping a spectrum of thought that encompasses a range of beliefs, skepticism, and imaginative possibilities regarding the feasibility of time travel. This chapter delves into the rich tapestry of divergent viewpoints, examining the nuances and complexities that define the diversity of thought on the tantalizing prospect of traversing the corridors of time.

Skeptical Realism: Navigating the Boundary Between Possibility and Impossibility:

At one end of the spectrum, we encounter the voices of skeptical realism—individuals who, while acknowledging the fascination with time travel, approach the concept with a cautious and critical lens. Skeptical realists contend that the challenges posed by the laws of physics, causality, and the limitations of human understanding render time travel inherently implausible.

Consider the arguments rooted in the principles of relativity, the conservation of energy, and the intricate complexities of causation. Skeptical realists assert that, despite the allure of temporal exploration, the fundamental constraints of the universe may impose insurmountable barriers to the realization of time travel. As we navigate this segment of the spectrum, it becomes evident that skeptical realism urges a pragmatic assessment of the theoretical and practical challenges that cast a shadow over the prospect of temporal journeys.

In exploring the diversity of thought on the possibility of time travel, individuals find themselves confronted with the reasoned skepticism of those who navigate the boundary between possibility and impossibility. The philosophical inquiry into skeptical realism becomes a reflection on the cautionary approach to temporal exploration and the recognition that acknowledging the limitations of our understanding is a crucial aspect of navigating the spectrum of thought.

Optimistic Pioneers: Embracing the Temporal Frontier with Unyielding Enthusiasm:

On the opposite end of the spectrum, we encounter the voices of optimistic pioneers—individuals who embrace the temporal frontier with unyielding enthusiasm and an unwavering belief in the eventual realization of time travel. Optimistic pioneers argue that as scientific understanding advances, technological innovations emerge, and our grasp of the cosmos deepens, the barriers that currently seem insurmountable may gradually yield to human ingenuity.

Consider the optimism rooted in the advancements of theoretical physics, the exploration of quantum phenomena, and the potential breakthroughs in energy generation. Optimistic pioneers envision a future where the mysteries of time can be unraveled, and the dream of temporal exploration becomes a tangible reality. As we navigate this segment of the spectrum, it becomes evident that optimistic pioneers fuel the imagination with a relentless pursuit of what may lie beyond the temporal horizon.

In exploring the diversity of thought on the possibility of time travel, individuals find themselves confronted with the boundless optimism of those who envision a future where the temporal frontier is conquered. The philosophical inquiry into optimistic pioneers becomes a reflection on the audacious spirit of those who dare to dream, pushing the boundaries of the imaginable and challenging the conventional narrative of temporal limitations.

Pragmatic Explorers: Balancing Possibility with Practicality:

Amidst the spectrum of thought, we encounter the voices of pragmatic explorers—individuals who navigate the terrain of temporal exploration with a balance of optimism and a grounding in practicality. Pragmatic explorers acknowledge the allure of time travel while remaining cognizant of the current scientific and technological limitations that pose formidable challenges.

Consider the pragmatic approach rooted in incremental advancements, step-by-step progress, and a commitment to realistic assessments of the temporal frontier. Pragmatic explorers advocate for a methodical exploration of the possibilities while actively engaging with the existing constraints, avoiding undue speculation and maintaining a focus on tangible advancements. As we navigate this segment of the spectrum, it becomes evident that pragmatic explorers seek a middle ground between optimism and skepticism, driven by a desire to balance the excitement of possibility with the pragmatism of the achievable.

In exploring the diversity of thought on the possibility of time travel, individuals find themselves confronted with the measured perspectives of those who seek to chart a course that respects the boundaries of current knowledge. The philosophical inquiry into pragmatic explorers becomes a reflection on the judicious navigation of the temporal landscape, emphasizing a thoughtful and realistic approach to the challenges and potential of temporal exploration.

Temporal Agnostics: Embracing the Mystery of the Unknowable:

Within the spectrum of thought, we encounter the voices of temporal agnostics—individuals who embrace the mystery of the unknowable and acknowledge the limitations of current understanding in unraveling the enigma of time. Temporal agnostics contend that, while the prospect of time travel is undeniably intriguing, the complexities inherent in the nature of time may forever elude complete comprehension.

Consider the agnostic stance rooted in humility before the vastness of the cosmos, the mysteries of fundamental physics, and the intricate nature of temporality. Temporal agnostics acknowledge that certain aspects of the temporal landscape may remain forever beyond the reach of human understanding, inviting a sense of wonder and humility in the face of the cosmic unknown. As we navigate this segment of the spectrum, it becomes evident that temporal agnostics find solace in embracing the perpetual mystery of time.

In exploring the diversity of thought on the possibility of time travel, individuals find themselves confronted with the contemplative perspectives of those who find comfort in the acceptance of the unknowable. The philosophical inquiry into temporal agnostics becomes a reflection on the humility that accompanies the recognition of our limitations and the acknowledgment that some mysteries may forever remain shrouded in the timeless veils of the cosmic unknown.

Conclusion: Navigating the Spectrum with Open Minds and Intellectual Curiosity:

As we navigate the spectrum of thought on the possibility of time travel, the voices of skeptical realism, optimistic pioneers, pragmatic explorers, and temporal agnostics resonate. The exploration of this diversity of thought highlights the intricacies of navigating the spectrum, each perspective contributing to the rich tapestry of human understanding. In the chapters that follow, we will continue our journey, delving into additional considerations that shape the frontiers of temporal exploration and redefine our perception of what may be achievable within the dynamic framework of the temporal landscape.

Conclusion
Summarizing key arguments against the possibility of time travel

As we embark on the culmination of our journey through the labyrinthine corridors of temporal exploration, it is imperative to cast a discerning eye on the key arguments against the tantalizing prospect of time travel. This concluding chapter seeks to distill the essence of skepticism, theoretical barriers, and practical constraints that collectively weave a tapestry of resistance against the realization of temporal journeys.

The Inescapable Grasp of Physics:

At the forefront of arguments against the possibility of time travel stands the inescapable grasp of physics—a formidable barrier that casts shadows on the fanciful dreams of traversing temporal landscapes. The principles of relativity, the conservation of energy, and the intricate dance of causality intertwine to form a complex web, restraining the whimsical notions of moving backward or forward in time.

Skeptics argue that the fundamental fabric of the universe, as described by the laws of physics, imposes insurmountable constraints. The very nature of time dilation, as outlined by Einstein's theory of relativity, underscores the challenges associated with achieving the speeds necessary to manipulate temporal progression. As we summarize the key arguments against time travel, the resolute grip of physics emerges as a formidable adversary, urging us to reconcile our temporal aspirations with the sobering realities dictated by the laws of the cosmos.

Causality: A Sentinel Against Temporal Trespass:

Embedded within the intricate tapestry of arguments against time travel is the sentinel of causality—a steadfast guardian that stands sentinel against temporal trespass. The interconnected web of cause and effect, woven into the very fabric of our reality, poses a formidable challenge to the whimsical notion of altering the past or glimpsing into the future.

Critics contend that the potential consequences of altering past events, encapsulated by the infamous grandfather paradox, serve as a cautionary tale. The implications of disrupting the delicate balance of causality echo through the corridors of philosophical inquiry, challenging the very foundations of our understanding of temporal progression. As we delve into the key arguments against time travel, the sentinel of causality emerges as a guardian, warning us of the perilous implications that may arise from tampering with the threads of cause and effect.

The Arrow of Time: A One-Way Journey:

A salient feature of the arguments against the possibility of time travel is the concept of the arrow of time—a one-way journey that defines the irreversibility of temporal progression. Critics posit that the asymmetry inherent in the flow of time, marked by the inexorable march from past to present to future, presents a formidable challenge to the whimsical notion of navigating backward along this unidirectional path.

The arrow of time, as manifested in the increase of entropy and the unfolding of events in a singular direction, stands as an enigma resistant to manipulation. Critics argue that the very essence of temporal experience is contingent on this irreversible flow, rendering the prospect of time travel into the past a paradoxical endeavor. As we synthesize the key arguments against time travel, the one-way nature of the arrow of time emerges as an immutable force, shaping the contours of temporal reality and resisting the whims of those who yearn to rewind the cosmic clock.

The Novikov Self-Consistency Principle: A Guardian of Temporal Integrity:

Integral to the arsenal of arguments against time travel is the Novikov self-consistency principle—an unwavering guardian that safeguards the integrity of temporal events. This principle, rooted in the realm of theoretical physics, postulates that any action or event undertaken by a time traveler is inherently constrained by the overarching principle of self-consistency.

Critics argue that the Novikov self-consistency principle serves as a safeguard against the creation of paradoxes, ensuring that any interaction with the past aligns seamlessly with the events that have transpired. This principle, rather than liberating temporal voyagers, imposes a strict set of rules, guiding their actions along a predestined path that upholds the coherence and consistency of the temporal narrative. As we distill the key arguments against time travel, the Novikov self-consistency principle emerges as a stern sentinel, vigilant in its defense of the temporal continuum.

Human Limitations: The Fragility of Temporal Aspirations:

Woven into the fabric of arguments against time travel is the frailty of human limitations—an acknowledgment that the very nature of our existence may render the realization of temporal journeys a distant and elusive prospect. Critics contend that the biological, psychological, and technological limitations inherent in the human condition pose insurmountable challenges to the whimsical dreams of temporal exploration.

The human body, fragile and susceptible to the ravages of time, may falter under the strains of temporal manipulation. Critics argue that the human mind, conditioned by the linear progression of temporal experience, may struggle to comprehend the intricacies of navigating non-linear paths. As we survey the key arguments against time travel, the specter of human limitations emerges as a poignant reminder of the fragility of our temporal aspirations, urging us to reconcile our dreams with the realities of our temporal existence.

Conclusion: Navigating the Abyss with Reverence and Humility:

As we navigate the abyss of arguments against the possibility of time travel, the resounding echoes of physics, causality, the arrow of time, the Novikov self-consistency principle, and human limitations reverberate. The synthesis of these key arguments forms a formidable fortress, urging us to approach the tantalizing prospect of temporal exploration with reverence and humility.

In concluding our exploration of the impossibility of time travel, it is essential to embrace the limitations that define the boundaries of our temporal existence. The very act of acknowledging these limitations, far from extinguishing the flame of curiosity, illuminates the path of intellectual humility. As we stand on the precipice of the temporal abyss, let us navigate with a deepened understanding of the cosmic intricacies that shape our journey through the enigmatic corridors of time.

Reinforcing the central thesis: Time travel, as commonly conceived, is not achievable

As we bring our expedition through the realms of temporal exploration to a close, it is paramount to drive home the central thesis that echoes through the corridors of skepticism, theoretical intricacies, and pragmatic realities: time travel, as commonly conceived, is not achievable. The journey we have undertaken, navigating the intricacies of physics, causality, the arrow of time, the Novikov self-consistency principle, and the limitations inherent in the human condition, converges to form a resounding declaration against the whimsical aspirations of temporal voyages.

Shattered Illusions: The Impossibility Within Our Grasp:

At the heart of our exploration lies the shattering of illusions—the dismantling of fanciful dreams that have permeated the collective consciousness. The journey through the theoretical, philosophical, and scientific landscapes has revealed a tapestry woven with threads of implausibility, cautionary principles, and insurmountable barriers. It is incumbent upon us to acknowledge that the very foundation upon which our fascination with time travel rests is fraught with challenges that transcend the boundaries of wishful thinking.

Critics argue that the allure of time travel, as commonly conceived in popular culture, arises from a blend of romanticized notions, scientific optimism, and a yearning to transcend the constraints of temporal existence. However, as we sift through the layers of illusion, we find that the whimsical dreams of traversing epochs and altering the course of history are anchored in a realm where reality and fantasy diverge.

Physics as the Sentinel of Impossibility:

At the forefront of the argument against the achievability of time travel stands the sentinel of physics—an immutable force that stands as a formidable barrier against the fanciful aspirations of temporal voyages. The principles of relativity, which have withstood the test of empirical validation, underscore the implausibility of achieving the speeds necessary to manipulate time. Critics assert that the very fabric of the universe, as dictated by the laws of physics, imposes constraints that transcend the reach of human ingenuity.

As we reinforce the central thesis, it becomes evident that the intricate dance of subatomic particles, the interplay of gravitational forces, and the unforgiving constraints of energy conservation collectively conspire to shatter the illusions that time travel, as commonly conceived, is within our grasp. The resolute grip of physics remains a sentinel, guarding the threshold of temporal exploration and urging us to approach the concept of time travel with a sober acknowledgment of our limitations.

Causality as the Bastion of Temporal Integrity:

Woven into the fabric of our exploration is the bastion of causality—a principle that stands resolute in safeguarding the integrity of temporal events. Critics argue that the very essence of temporal progression is intertwined with the web of cause and effect, presenting a formidable challenge to the whimsical notion of altering the past or venturing into the future.

As we reinforce the central thesis, the sentinel of causality emerges as a guardian, resisting the impulse to tamper with the delicate threads that weave the tapestry of temporal reality. The implications of disrupting the intricate balance of cause and effect, encapsulated by the grandfather paradox and similar conundrums, serve as cautionary tales, warning us of the perilous consequences that may arise from temporal trespass. The shattering of illusions demands a respectful acknowledgment of the unyielding nature of causality, urging us to navigate the temporal landscape with an understanding of the intricacies that define our existence.

The Arrow of Time as an Unyielding Force:

Integral to our synthesis is the recognition of the arrow of time—a one-way journey that defines the irreversibility of temporal progression. Critics contend that the asymmetry inherent in the flow of time, marked by the inexorable march from past to present to future, poses a formidable challenge to the whimsical notion of navigating backward along this unidirectional path.

As we reinforce the central thesis, the one-way nature of the arrow of time emerges as an unyielding force, resistant to manipulation or deviation. The increase of entropy, the unfolding of events in a singular direction, and the intrinsic features of our temporal experience collectively form a barrier against the illusions of rewinding the cosmic clock. The shattering of illusions demands a recognition of the constraints imposed by the arrow of time, urging us to navigate the temporal abyss with an acceptance of the one-way journey that defines our existence.

The Novikov Self-Consistency Principle as a Stern Sentinel:

Embedded within our exploration is the Novikov self-consistency principle—a sentinel that stands as a stern guardian, upholding the coherence and consistency of the temporal continuum. Critics argue that rather than liberating temporal voyagers, this principle imposes a set of rules that guide their actions along a predestined path.

As we reinforce the central thesis, the Novikov self-consistency principle emerges as a stern sentinel, vigilant in its defense of the temporal narrative. The recognition that any interaction with the past aligns seamlessly with the events that have transpired demands a sober acknowledgment of the constraints that govern temporal exploration. The shattering of illusions invites us to navigate the corridors of time with a recognition of the principles that safeguard the temporal continuum.

Human Limitations: The Inherent Fragility of Aspirations:

Integral to the synthesis is the acknowledgment of human limitations—an understanding that the very nature of our existence may render the realization of temporal journeys a distant and elusive prospect. Critics argue that the biological, psychological, and technological constraints inherent in the human condition pose insurmountable challenges to the whimsical dreams of temporal exploration.

As we reinforce the central thesis, the specter of human limitations emerges as a poignant reminder of the fragility of our temporal aspirations. The recognition that the human body may falter, the human mind may struggle to comprehend non-linear paths, and our technological prowess may be insufficient demands a humble acknowledgment of the constraints that define our temporal existence. The shattering of illusions invites us to approach the concept of time travel with a reverent awareness of our limitations.

Embracing the Impossibility: A Call to Intellectual Humility:

In reinforcing the central thesis that time travel, as commonly conceived, is not achievable, we are called to embrace the impossibility with intellectual humility. The shattering of illusions demands a recognition of the complex interplay of forces—physics, causality, the arrow of time, the Novikov self-consistency principle, and human limitations—

that collectively form an impregnable fortress against the whims of temporal voyages.

As we stand at the crossroads of fantasy and reality, let us navigate the abyss of temporal exploration with a profound acknowledgment of the impossibility that defines our temporal landscape. The shattering of illusions invites us to approach the concept of time travel not with despair, but with a deepened understanding of the cosmic intricacies that shape our journey through the enigmatic corridors of time. The central thesis reverberates as a call to intellectual humility, urging us to explore the mysteries of existence with a reverence for the boundaries that define our temporal reality.

Encouraging readers to appreciate the imaginative aspect of time travel while recognizing its implausibility

As we conclude our journey through the labyrinth of temporal speculation, it is paramount to extend an invitation to our readers—a call to appreciate the imaginative allure of time travel while simultaneously recognizing its implausibility. The exploration of the impossibility of time travel need not be a funeral dirge for fanciful dreams but rather a celebration of the human capacity for imagination, creativity, and intellectual curiosity.

The Canvas of Imagination: Painting Temporal Landscapes with Dreams:

At the heart of our conclusion lies an invitation to embrace the boundless canvas of imagination—an arena where the brushstrokes of dreams paint temporal landscapes that defy the constraints of reality. The human capacity to conceive of temporal voyages, alter historical trajectories, and transcend the limitations of linear progression is a testament to the richness of our imaginative faculties.

As we encourage readers to appreciate the imaginative aspect of time travel, we celebrate the myriad narratives, speculative fiction, and artistic expressions that have woven intricate tapestries of temporal exploration. From the pages of literature to the screens of cinema, the canvas of imagination unfurls vistas of possibility that beckon us to explore the timeless realms of what-if scenarios and alternate realities.

Navigating the Sea of Speculation: Voyages Beyond the Horizon of the Possible:

Our readers are invited to embark on voyages beyond the horizon of the possible, navigating the sea of speculation with a sense of wonder and intellectual curiosity. While the central thesis asserts the implausibility of time travel as commonly conceived, it need not extinguish the flames of curiosity that illuminate the path of speculative inquiry.

Consider the diverse narratives that have dared to challenge the boundaries of temporal limitation—stories that traverse epochs, bend the fabric of reality, and invite readers to suspend disbelief. From H.G. Wells' "The Time Machine" to contemporary works that continue to explore the temporal frontier, the sea of speculation offers an ocean of narratives that invite us to revel in the imaginative possibilities that emerge when the implausible becomes the playground of creativity.

The Interplay of Science and Fiction: Bridging Realities and Fantasies:

In encouraging readers to appreciate the imaginative aspect of time travel, we recognize the symbiotic relationship between science and fiction. The interplay of these realms serves as a bridge between the realities of scientific understanding and the fantastical realms of speculative fiction. While the implausibility of time travel is rooted in the constraints of physics and causality, fiction provides a space where these constraints can be temporarily suspended, allowing the human mind to soar into realms unfettered by the limitations of our temporal existence.

Readers are invited to explore the works of visionaries who have seamlessly woven scientific concepts into the fabric of fiction, creating narratives that spark the imagination while acknowledging the implausibility of the scenarios presented. The interplay of science and fiction becomes a tapestry that enriches our understanding of both realms, fostering an appreciation for the creative synthesis of knowledge and imagination.

Temporal Voyages as Thought Experiments: Exploring the What-If Realms:

Consider the notion of temporal voyages not as literal endeavors but as thought experiments that transcend the boundaries of the achievable. In the realm of speculative inquiry, readers are encouraged to engage with the what-if scenarios that temporal exploration presents. What if we could witness historical events firsthand? What if we could alter the course of our own lives? These questions, while tethered to the implausibility of realization, serve as springboards for intellectual exploration and philosophical contemplation.

Readers are invited to participate in the mental gymnastics of thought experiments, navigating the corridors of hypothetical scenarios that challenge our preconceptions and provoke introspection. The implausibility of turning these thought experiments into tangible experiences does not diminish their value but, rather, enhances their role as catalysts for intellectual curiosity and reflection.

The Pleasure of Cognitive Dissonance: Holding Contradictory Notions with Delight:

As we encourage readers to appreciate the imaginative aspect of time travel, we delve into the pleasure of cognitive dissonance—the capacity to hold contradictory notions with delight. The acknowledgment of the implausibility of time travel need not extinguish the joy derived from entertaining the fantastical possibilities that emerge from the recesses of the human mind.

Readers are invited to revel in the joy of paradox, embracing the simultaneous acceptance of the implausible and the appreciation for the imaginative narratives that arise from the juxtaposition of contradictory ideas. The pleasure of cognitive dissonance becomes a source of intellectual stimulation, prompting us to navigate the tension between what is known and what is imagined with a sense of playful curiosity.

Temporal Fantasies as Cultural Artifacts: Appreciating the Tapestry of Human Creativity:

Temporal fantasies, whether expressed through literature, art, cinema, or other cultural mediums, serve as cultural artifacts that enrich the tapestry of human creativity. In encouraging readers to appreciate the imaginative aspect of time travel, we celebrate these cultural contributions as expressions of the human spirit's relentless pursuit of exploration and understanding.

Consider the impact of temporal fantasies on popular culture—the way in which these narratives shape societal narratives, influence collective perceptions, and become integral components of our shared mythos. From iconic time-traveling characters to narratives that explore the consequences of temporal interference, these cultural artifacts invite readers to participate in a collective conversation about the nature of time, the possibilities of alternate realities, and the imaginative frontiers that continue to captivate our collective consciousness.

A Call to Intellectual Openness: Navigating the Paradoxes with Reverence:

In encouraging readers to appreciate the imaginative aspect of time travel, we issue a call to intellectual openness—an invitation to navigate the paradoxes with reverence rather than despair. The recognition of implausibility need not be a barrier but, rather, a threshold that invites readers to engage with the complexities of temporal exploration with a sense of wonder and humility.

Consider the paradoxes that emerge from the juxtaposition of imagination and implausibility as gateways to intellectual exploration. The recognition that the human mind can conceive of scenarios that defy the constraints of reality becomes a testament to the vastness of our cognitive landscape. As readers navigate the paradoxes with reverence, they are empowered to appreciate the imaginative aspect of time travel while acknowledging its implausibility as a canvas upon which the human mind paints the murals of speculative inquiry.

Conclusion: A Tapestry Woven with Dreams and Realities:

As we conclude our exploration, readers are invited to reflect on the tapestry woven with dreams and realities—a tapestry that celebrates the imaginative allure of time travel while recognizing its implausibility. The journey through the theoretical, philosophical, and scientific landscapes need not be a march towards disillusionment but, rather, a dance that harmonizes the whims of the human imagination with the sobering realities of our temporal existence.

In the concluding moments of our exploration, readers are encouraged to carry with them the appreciation for the imaginative aspect of time travel as a lantern that illuminates the corridors of intellectual curiosity. The tapestry, enriched by the threads of speculative inquiry and creative expression, becomes a testament to the ceaseless pursuit of understanding that defines the human spirit.

As we step away from the enigmatic realms of temporal exploration, let the echoes of our journey linger—a reminder that the implausibility of time travel need not extinguish the flames of curiosity but, rather, serve as a catalyst for the perpetual dance between dreams and realities. In the tapestry of human intellectual endeavor, the appreciation for the imaginative aspect of time travel becomes a vibrant thread that weaves its way through the annals of history, inviting future generations to engage with the mysteries that continue to captivate the human mind.

THE END

Glossary

Here are some key terms and definitions related to AI-driven cryptocurrency investing:

1. ChronoFallacy: The misconception or false belief in the feasibility of time travel, debunked by scientific and philosophical constraints.

2. Temporal Voyages: Hypothetical journeys through time, often explored in literature and film, but deemed implausible in reality.

3. Impossibility: The state of being unable to occur or exist, highlighting the inherent limitations preventing time travel.

4. Scientific Constraints: The boundaries imposed by established principles of physics and cosmology, challenging the viability of time travel.

5. Causality: The principle that events are interconnected through cause and effect, posing challenges to altering past events.

6. Arrow of Time: The unidirectional progression of time from past to present to future, resisting reversal or manipulation.

7. Novikov Self-Consistency Principle: The concept that any action taken in the past must align with the existing timeline, restricting changes.

8. Human Limitations: Inherent constraints on the human body, mind, and technology, hindering practical time travel endeavors.

9. Thought Experiments: Mental exercises exploring hypothetical scenarios, offering insights into the philosophical implications of time travel.

10. Intellectual Humility: Acknowledging the limits of human understanding and embracing a modest approach to the complexities of time.

11. Cognitive Dissonance: Holding contradictory beliefs simultaneously, as experienced when appreciating the imaginative aspect of time travel alongside its acknowledged implausibility.

12. Temporal Fantasies: Creative expressions, including literature and art, depicting fanciful scenarios of time travel, often rooted in cultural exploration.

13. Paradoxes: Seemingly contradictory situations arising from the juxtaposition of imagination and implausibility in the context of time travel.

14. Intellectual Openness: A mindset encouraging receptivity to diverse ideas, even when grappling with the paradoxes of time travel concepts.

15. Tapestry of Dreams and Realities: The intricate fabric woven by the interplay of human imagination with the acknowledged implausibility of time travel, shaping cultural narratives and intellectual exploration.

Potential References

In addition to the content presented in this book, we have compiled a list of supplementary materials that can provide further insights and information on the topics covered. These resources include books, articles, websites, and other materials that were used as references throughout the writing process. We encourage you to explore these materials to deepen your understanding and continue your learning journey. Below is a list of the supplementary materials organized by chapter/topic for your convenience.

Introduction:

Greene, Brian. "The Fabric of the Cosmos: Space, Time, and the Texture of Reality." Vintage, 2005.

Thorne, Kip S. "Black Holes and Time Warps: Einstein's Outrageous Legacy." W. W. Norton & Company, 1994.

Davies, Paul. "How to Build a Time Machine." Penguin Books, 2002.

Chapter 1: Exploring Theoretical Constraints:

Hawking, Stephen. "A Brief History of Time." Bantam Books, 1988.

Kaku, Michio. "Hyperspace: A Scientific Odyssey Through Parallel Universes, Time Warps, and the Tenth Dimension." Anchor, 1995.

Barrow, John D. "The Book of Universes: Exploring the Limits of the Cosmos." W. W. Norton & Company, 2012.

Chapter 2: Philosophical Considerations:

Lewis, David. "On the Plurality of Worlds." Blackwell, 1986.

Smart, J. J. C. "Free Will, Praise, and Blame." Mind, Vol. 70, No. 279, 1961, pp. 291-306.

Sider, Theodore. "Four-Dimensionalism: An Ontology of Persistence and Time." Oxford University Press, 2001.

Chapter 3: Scientific Challenges:

Everett III, Hugh. "Relative State Formulation of Quantum Mechanics." Reviews of Modern Physics, Vol. 29, No. 3, 1957, pp. 454-462.

Alcubierre, Miguel. "The warp drive: hyper-fast travel within general relativity." Classical and Quantum Gravity, Vol. 11, No. 5, 1994, pp. L73-L77.

Davies, Paul. "How to Build a Time Machine." Penguin Books, 2002.

Chapter 4: Historical Impact:

Gleick, James. "Time Travel: A History." Pantheon, 2016.

Jha, Alok. "The Physics of Time: The Mind-Blowing Science of How Time Works." Penguin, 2018.

Fara, Patricia. "Pandora's Breeches: Women, Science and Power in the Enlightenment." Pimlico, 2004.

Chapter 5: Human Limitations:

Kurzweil, Ray. "The Singularity Is Near: When Humans Transcend Biology." Penguin Books, 2005.

Dvorsky, George. "Will Biological Immortality Ever Be Possible?" io9, 2015. Link

Harari, Yuval Noah. "Sapiens: A Brief History of Humankind." Harper, 2014.

Chapter 6: Alternative Perspectives:

Tegmark, Max. "Our Mathematical Universe: My Quest for the Ultimate Nature of Reality." Knopf, 2014.

Carroll, Sean. "From Eternity to Here: The Quest for the Ultimate Theory of Time." Dutton, 2010.

Davies, Paul. "The Goldilocks Enigma: Why Is the Universe Just Right for Life?" Mariner Books, 2007.

Conclusion:

Carroll, Sean. "The Big Picture: On the Origins of Life, Meaning, and the Universe Itself." Dutton, 2016.

Penrose, Roger. "The Emperor's New Mind: Concerning Computers, Minds, and the Laws of Physics." Oxford University Press, 1989.

Kuhn, Thomas S. "The Structure of Scientific Revolutions." University of Chicago Press, 1962.

www.ingramcontent.com/pod-product-compliance
Lightning Source LLC
LaVergne TN
LVHW010322070526
838199LV00065B/5636